FAITH AND FACT

Faith and Fact

A Guide to Economics Through Christian Understanding

by

ALFRED P. HAAKE

THE STACKPOLE COMPANY

Harrisburg, Pennsylvania

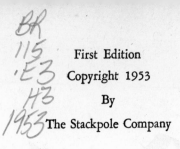

Printed in the U. S. A.

THE TELEGRAPH PRESS

Established 1831

Harrisburg, Pennsylvania

To
My Sainted Mother
and
My Beloved Wife

INTRODUCTION

The purpose of an introduction is to introduce the reader to the author and to the contents of his book.

I am conferring a favor on you, the reader, by introducing you to Alfred P. Haake, Ph.D. I speak out of personal experience, for having known Dr. Haake for many years, I can testify that he is one of the most sincere, inspiring, genuine and lovable persons whom it is my honor to call a friend. His activities have covered many fields; that of clergyman, university professor, business man, author, lecturer and mayor of his home town of Park Ridge, Illinois. He is scholarly by nature and can more than hold his own in any gathering of intellectuals. He is versed in their ways, talks their language and shares their delight in learning. His mind is easily distinguished in any gathering of scholarly men, however eminent that group may be. Among some there prevails the curious notion that only radicals are the true scholars. Dr. Haake explodes that false idea for he is so profoundly competent in scholarship, his grounds of opinion and conviction are so certain that I would have great sympathy for any person who would attempt to confound or confuse him.

However, I do not wish to picture him as a clever matcher of wits; he is far too genuine, too deep in his sincerity to be thus characterized. He is an earnest seeker after truth. He repudiates the false, the specious, the compromise, the double thought, the half-truth, the white lie. His clean, honest, Christian mind is content only with the truth. You can always be sure that anything he writes or says is true to the best of his knowledge and conviction. As a true scholar he is judicial in manner, temperate in expression, humble in attitude, kindly in reaction to those who disagree or oppose, but always sturdy and indomitable in defense of principles he believes to be right.

Dr. Haake is a man of gentle nature. There is a saintliness about him in his relationship to God and his fellow men. I have known few men who more devoutly follow Jesus Christ day by day. He early learned the power of faith. As a young boy he stuttered badly. He suffered the thoughtless but cruel jibes of his schoolmates because of this affliction. One Sunday afternoon in the Chicago Central Y.M.C.A. he listened to a speech by the late Senator Albert W. Beveridge who told his youthful listeners that God would give them power to overcome any difficulty if they would believe and be faithful.

Young Haake often went to the shore of the lake and filled his mouth with pebbles after the manner of Demosthenes, so anxious was he to speak. In his agony he would fall on the ground and pray, "Oh God, let me talk." Today he is one of the most eloquent and convincing speakers on the American platform.

He believes in America as a land of freedom and opportunity. He believes that God and Jesus Christ are the source of freedom and the true foundation of this nation. He is a lover of people, especially those who, like himself, must struggle against great odds. He believes in the value of struggle against adversity. Why shouldn't he? It gave him the great strength, the deep understanding, the kindliness which endears him to his host of friends.

You will form a friendship with a great soul as you learn to know the author of this book.

As to the book itself it is a veritable library of basic economic knowledge. Moreover, it is written so plainly and clearly that even I can understand it. It is hard to think of a book on economics as being "thrilling," for ordinarily it seems dull (at least to me), but this book is actually fascinating. Most people today are reading economics constantly in magazines and newspapers, and not a few are talking economics, forming and expressing opinions. Tragically such reading and talking is often done with pitifully inadequate knowledge of the subject. Perhaps this explains much of the unsound economic philosophy and practice which plagues the United States today.

Everyone who wants to understand the origin, meaning and application of economic ideas and principles will find Dr. Haake's book tremendously helpful and valuable.

And of even greater importance the author traces the relationship of economics to faith. The connection of religion to the laws of production, distribution, price and profit is developed in a manner both sound and fascinating. I will go so far as to say that I do not see how any clergyman can fail to own and study this book. For the layman, those who seek to serve God and country and no less those whose purpose reaches no higher than personal happiness and success, this book is a true aid and challenge.

All that I can say is—get the book. Do not miss this stimulating and richly satisfying reading and study experience. I also suggest that the book be made available for young people's discussion groups. Offer it on church book tables. Recommend it to your friends. Here is the greatest book of our time on Christian economics. It is in this field that the great spiritual and ethical principles are being tested and the future being formed.

In this vastly important struggle Alfred P. Haake is a safe and inspiring guide and his great work, "Faith and Fact," is the most important text book.

Norman Vincent Peale

Marble Collegiate Church
Fifth Avenue and 29th Street
New York City

PREFACE

This book is the fruition of life-long effort to discover the practicality of religion, or faith, in dealing with basic economics, or fact, problems that arise out of making a living and living as a member of society.

It is written for religious leaders, clergy and laymen, to offer them a simple and helpful explanation of economics, to facilitate their use of economic facts in the structure of applied religion and ethics. The religious leader can exert tremendous influence on the thinking of people and it is important that he provide himself with economic truth not ordinarily available in the course of his work.

It is written for laymen who seek to reconcile the basic truths of religion with the basic facts of economics, and so fortify themselves in applying the truths of religion in the making of a living.

During half a century of active business and professional experience, the author has learned that the ultimate answers to most of the problems of living are found in the field of religion. What men believe, determines ultimately what they do. It is faith grown out of fact that leads us to better understanding of fact and in turn to factually justified faith.

It is the author's conviction that Christianity is the most practical of all religions as a guide to living because its truths and principles fit into all fields of research, knowledge, and endeavor. If we understood the basic truths of both religion and economics, we could apply religious principles in the winning of success, and so contribute to the permanent betterment of mankind.

For almost two thousand years we have had the teachings of Jesus and in them the answers to most of our problems. We need to avail ourselves of those teachings, to strengthen and encourage the leadership of those devout disciples who give their lives to the dissemination of religious truth and principle.

To the friends who have borne with me and the audiences who have listened to me through the years in which I developed the thinking of this book, I am deeply grateful for their patience, constructive criticisms, and helpful reactions. It is my hope and prayer that I may have contributed somewhat to a better understanding of the fundamental agreements in religion and economics and their application to personal growth and fulfilment in dealing with daily problems.

Alfred P. Haake

Park Ridge, Ill., January, 1953

CONTENTS

PART IV. TRIUMPH OF FAITH IN FACT

PART ONE - RELIGION

(A Basis for FAITH and Understanding of FACT)

RELIGION: *A set or system of beliefs built out of the awareness or conviction of a supreme being with a divine purpose in creation and continuing control through the exercise or implementation of the Will of that being. We call the being God.*

FAITH: *Acceptance of the beliefs we call religion and the fact of God as arbiter, as criteria by which the individual human being regulates or governs his conduct. Religion is in the realm of faith, and becomes fact when individual conduct follows its precepts.*

FACT: *The quality of being actual, or what has actual existence. Thus, economics is in the realm of fact because it has to do with activities and resulting relationships and institutions of man, which arise out of his efforts to make a living. But, faith is needed to make fact effective.*

Therefore, the reconciliation, or adjustment, of faith and fact, or religion and economics, becomes a pattern of conduct on which the individual risks his life and possessions.

CHAPTER 1

ORIGINS

O NE of the most important problems of our time is the coordination of religion and economics. Neither is too well or widely
understood, and the relationship between them is more of a mystery
than it should or need be. Many believe that the two are in conflict,
either seeing business as corrupt and materialistic, or finding no help
for the harrassed industrialist in the impotent teachings of impractical
religionists. Still others would go so far as to lay upon the church
responsibility for itself seeking out the solutions to economic problems
through uneconomic urges and motives, or would so modify our competitive enterprise system as to bring all economic activities under
control of a central government.

It is my conviction, grown out of years of endeavor to live the
decent life in profession and business, that there is no necessary conflict between religion and economics. Rightly understood, we can
reconcile both in solving many of the problems which now bedevil
our efforts to improve the well-being of mankind.

Of vital importance is the fact that both religion and economics
are indespensable to life and have grown out of the needs of developing man. The principles that govern in one are no less important in
the other. We must learn what those principles, or laws, are.

WHAT IS RELIGION?

Religion began with understanding, in man's emancipation from the
mathematical, chemical and physical forces that controlled him as an
animal; as he became aware of himself as an individual in his sur-
roundings. He saw one event follow another, sequences repeated. Thus,
he saw the sun rise in the morning and go down at night, day after
day, except when clouds shut the sun from his sight. He felt the
winds, the rains always made him wet. He learned to relate cold and
warmth, hunger and weariness to recurring phenomena, and arrived
at a conception of what we would call the law of cause and effect.

Back of the casual events he recognized the existence of some power
or person, powers or persons, greater than himself, to whose whim
or will he was subject without recourse. And it was only natural that

the man would strive to please or propitiate that power. There we have the beginnings of religion in the life of man. The fact that early efforts to please or appease that power took the form of magic and the rites of sorcerers is indication that understanding had not yet risen to adequate grasp of the nature of Deity; but it was still a crude form of religion in that it recognized a power that controls life and matter and that must be worshipped if man would live.

In his quest for understanding of the relationship between himself and Deity, man sought explanation in the genesis of the world in which he lives. It is interesting that a thousand centuries of discovery and reflection have not yet given us the complete answer. Man is still baffled in his search for proof of the beginning of things. If we accept evolution, by whatever name we call it, we must at once concede that there has been change and development from one form to another. As the record shows, the change is from simple to complex by a process of division and subdivision, with ensuing specialization of function out of undifferentiated functions. From this pattern of change it must be apparent that the process reaches back toward a time of less and less complex forms and ultimately a single undifferentiated mass of matter, inorganic chaos.

What transpired before the fact of that undifferentiated inorganic matter is still a mystery to man. Whence it came and how we do not and probably cannot, with our finite limitations, ever know. The concept is too stupendous for human understanding. It is enough that we can begin with that undifferentiated mass of matter. From there on we have the terse and concise story of creation as found in the first chapter of the Bible.

GOD IN THE BEGINNING

"In the beginning God created the heaven and the earth. And the earth was without form and void; and darkness was upon the face of the deep. And the Spirit of God moved upon the face of the waters. And God said, Let there be light; and there was light."

Then He divided the light from the darkness and created day and night. He separated the firmament from the waters and made the heavens. He gathered the waters togther and let the dry land appear, separating earth and the seas. The earth brought forth vegetation, which multiplied after its kind. Then came the stars, the sun and moon in their places. The waters became populated with living creatures, fowls appeared on the earth nourished by the vegetation. Then other living creatures, cattle, creeping things and beasts of all kinds, each multiplying after his kind.

And the crowning achievement!

"So God created man in His own image, . . . male and female created He them . . . And God blessed them, and God said unto them, Be fruitful and multiply, and replenish the earth, and subdue it: and have dominion over the fish of the sea, and over every living thing that moveth upon the earth."

Thus, the Lord God, having formed man of the dust of the ground, breathed into his nostrils the breath of life: *"and man became a living soul."* His span of life later completed, man's body would return to the earth as it was, but his spirit, the living soul, would return to God who gave it.

"And God saw everything that he had
made, and, behold, it was very good."

There are stories and legends from other sources which contribute similar explanations of the beginnings of the world we know, whatever may be the significance of that fact. But the story does not rely for its authenticity only on the fact that it is found in a Book. It is also in accord with the broad discoveries and findings of science. The story is a poetic and inspired condensation of what would require many pages of scientific explanation and detail, but it stands.

Even the once-feared hypotheses and conclusions of Darwin, with their threat to still unripe religious understanding, opened the way to a more complete and majestic grasp of the truth. Science has become the handmaiden of religion and helped us to learn that there can be no satisfactory explanation of the world in which we live, except in God and Divine Purpose with His Will implemented in the laws that govern the universe. The Story in the Book has been substantiated by facts of the universe as unfolded in developing science.

Through long centuries man has sought to establish his dominion over all other living things, to subdue the earth on which he was placed. The record of that struggle is the story we call history, some of it recorded in the rocks and layers of geological formations, and latterly in those writings and evidences of the life of man which have survived the ravages of war and passing of time.

Through those same centuries man's idea of God has undergone change and development, but the two inseparable ideas of a religion have gone on, expanding recognition of the sequence of events and belief in a power that controls or directs that sequence and, with it, the course of nature and human life.

Out of association of those two ideas comes the premise that there is a moral force and purpose in the universe. There is increasing evidence of a plan for the world; that the plan grows or evolves through the centuries as does any flower, tree or other thing, animate or inanimate, according to the immutable laws that govern the universe. Man can interfere with the workings of the plan, and perhaps even delay or hasten its fulfilment for an infinitesimal fraction of eternity, but the plan moves on, and man determines his own fate by the degree to which he cooperates with or opposes the Will of the Creator operating in the plan.

THE IDEA OF GOD

Primitive man sought protection in a gallery of gods. One ruled the air, another the waters, still another hurled thunder and lightning. The very trees and rocks housed spirits whose good-will was deemed necessary to life in the primitive efforts of man to propitiate the more important of his imagined demons and friendly spirits. He even conceived that many of these gods, spirits and demons, had their own dissensions and struggles among themselves for power over man and the universe.

Into this pagan world, a world futile and without purpose came the discovery of one supreme God. This discovery, not limited to any one people or area, appeared in numerous places with as many variations as there were peoples who conceived the idea. But among them, from the records available to us, it appears that the patriarch of modern faith was one Abram, later called Abraham. Father of the Jews and progenitor of their race, he gave to his descendants the concept of one God, a God of truth, order and justice. And he called His name Jehovah.

The concept of one God was tremendously significant. Recognition of that God, eternal, as Creator of the universe, Ruler of all, Supreme Judge and Arbiter of the conduct and destiny of man, lifted man from under the tyranny of perverse, fickle and unreasonable demons and spirits, and fitted him into an orderly pattern of law according to which he might safely regulate his conduct.

THE LAWS OF GOD

For man to live in obedience to that God, it was necessary that His Will be revealed to man in laws or admonitions by which man could govern or guide his conduct. Here again, in various parts of the world, growing out of man's dawning understanding of the Creator and out of his own needs as an individual, and a member of groups, came the basic laws of life. They are common to all the great faiths surviving today, though phrased differently. The most widely known and accepted of them all grew out of the basic law of life as learned by Abraham and were later codified in the greatest document ever given to man, the Ten Commandments of Moses.

The first of these commandments is the basis and substance of them all. God is recognized as the Author of the universe, beside Whom no other God may be raised. Man receives all from God. With life he is given freedom, the right to choose for himself how he will use his energies, abilities and opportunities. He is permitted even the right to choose between the acceptance and rejection of the God who gave him the right. And he is held responsible for the choices he makes and the consequences that flow from them.

Being given the authority and the power, the command to subdue the earth, be fruitful and multiply, to gain dominion over all other creatures and to earn his bread in the sweat of his face, the opportunity thus given to man becomes his responsibility and stewardship. And now, with the Ten Commandments he is given the admonitions by which he is to guide his conduct in relation to God and to his fellow man.

It is significant that only two of the commandments, to keep the sabbath day holy and to honor our parents, are stated positively. The rest are in the negative or "shalt-nots." We are *not to have any other gods before Him, not to worship any idols or graven images, nor to take His name in vain.* We are *forbidden to kill, to commit adultery, to steal or bear false witness.* And finally we are *warned against covetousness in any of its forms with relation to possessions of any other human being.* The significance lies in the fact that we are thus given limitations within which our freedom may be exercised. We may choose to do within these limitations what we will, without invoking the wrath of the Almighty, thus giving man a much more dignified position than could be his if specific rules were laid for every possible form of behavior or individual act. Truth, order and justice are established as the pattern of behavior within which man must work out his own destiny.

But man is still the animal which emerged from the muck of chaos. Through many centuries of evolution he responded to the forces of physics, chemistry and mathematical chance. With the breathing of conscience into the creature He thus developed, the Creator set in motion the higher evolution of moral and spiritual being. This higher evolution or growth would come through the individual's mastery of himself in obedience to God. But the pull of the lower man back toward his animal origins has always made it difficult for man to follow the commandments, or even to recognize fully the wisdom of following them. He needed more than admonition. He needed a living example.

Son of God

Into one of the catastrophic eras of man's development, while nations rose and fell in the quest for power, came a humble artisan whose faith in the teachings of His forebears was so great that He gave himself literally and wholly to the service of God. He demonstrated with and in His own life the rightness of the teachings of obedience to God and the possibility of living by those teachings. He was one of many who have served us so through the ages, but He came closer to the ultimate than did any of the rest. He breathed new life into dust-ridden precepts more honored by the negligence than the observance of man. He was of God and God was in Him.

Jesus of Nazareth came to fulfil the law of Moses and to lift the concept of God out of the anthropomorphic cast into which the materialistic yearnings of man had permitted that concept to gravitate. He taught us that God is a Spirit and must be worshipped in spirit and in truth. He taught that life is more than meat, that spirit is more than material and that it is through mastery of the material yearnings and needs within himself that man can evolve toward the higher moral and spiritual levels of being.

To Truth, Order and Justice, Jesus added Love as the great impelling force in the world. In Matthew 22, verses 37 to 40, Jesus thus crowned His teachings:

> "Jesus said unto him, Thou shalt love the Lord thy God with all thy heart, and with all thy soul, and with all thy mind. This is the first and great commandment. And the second is like unto it, Thou shalt love thy neighbor as thyself. On these two commandments hang all the law and all the prophets."

Jesus oriented this love first toward God and His purpose, and then toward man as the agent of God in evolving the plan. He saw man worshipping and serving God through serving his fellow-man, and the two great laws have come to their epitome in what is universally known as the Golden Rule, "Do unto others as you would have others do unto you." The highest good on earth becomes man's realization of himself as God had ordained. The ultimate good, toward which moral and spiritual evolution carries man, is Oneness with God. Atonement becomes at-one-ment.

Through these teachings are established obedience and self-realization as basis for man's relationship to God, mutual consideration or neighborliness as basis for relations with his fellow-man, and stewardship as man's responsibility for the physical world in which he lives.

The Russian Tolstoy epitomized these truths in a beautiful story. In his searching for truth, the philosopher came upon an uncultured peasant by a roadside. He asked the peasant, "Why do we live?" The untutored peasant, surprised that so wise a man should ask so foolish a question, replied, "We live that we may serve God."

The immortal Ghandi, non-Christian in sect but Christ-like in spirit, lived literally the teachings of religion for the life of man. It is impossible to measure the far-reaching influence of his personality and spirit over the years in which he lived and those yet to come.

IN PRACTICE

Yet, religion is far from the force it should be in the development of civilization. It is impossible to direct each and every man personally or to bring him into accord with the principles by which we know we should live. We dare not trust individual conscience without limit or guidance. Leaders are needed to help man understand and accept a sound basis and method for living. What the Golden Rule means in terms of individual rights and responsibilities, how men should share the goods of the earth and how those shares should be determined, are still roots of most of the world's most distressing problems. Out of the differences of opinion and clash of interest, inherent in the nature of man, have come work and play, war and peace, greed and generosity, inhumanity and self-sacrifice, hate and love and all the host of ideals and practices in which man engages during his life on earth.

Among these practices are those which we include in what is called economics. Economics is really a part of the over-all pattern of human behavior with which religion is concerned. Economic behavior includes all the acts man performs in the process of subduing the earth, gaining dominion over other creatures, in short, the process of making a living.

To the extent that there is conflict in the process of economics with what are deemed the principles of religion, it is due to lack of understanding and the fact that most men still need to be convinced that there is no contradiction between the faith of religion and the facts of economics. The Ten Commandments, it is said, are admonitions given in the name of a God, but what needs to be shown is that the laws which govern the material world and the processes necessary for man to wring a living from that world are in harmony with spiritual and divine truths as revealed in religion.

We must be able to show that the code of conduct with which religion provides man as the measure by which to guide his activities, the rules of the game in relation to other human beings, also squares with the facts and laws of the physical world in which man lives. Upon those of us who believe that this same religious code grown out of the laws of Moses and the teachings of Jesus, is truly universal and provides the common denominator by which men of all nations could live in peace and amity with each other, upon those of us who so believe falls the challenge to reconcile those teachings with practical considerations in dealing with material facts and forces.

It is toward that end that the next chapter presents an analysis of the basic laws of life, found operative in the life of man as a creature on earth.

CHAPTER 2

BASIC LAWS OF LIFE

THE laws which govern the material world, laws of chemistry, physics, biology, economics and the rest, like the laws that govern life, are neither moral nor immoral. They are statements of principles or of relationships of cause and effect, but are themselves free of any color of morality. The motives and purposes of the individual human being who evokes or utilizes any law may be moral or immoral, but that quality is in the individual human being and not in the law involved.

Thus, one may use the figure of 50% to be added to a quantity. That is merely a mathematical process in accord with a law or principle. But, if the 50% be added to a dose of poison to make it lethal the purpose may be pronounced as immoral because it tends toward crime, whereas the same mathematical process, applied to increasing the salary of a deserving worker, characterizes the purpose as moral.

The term moral, or immoral, goes immediately back to the choice we make as between a universe governed by blind forces or a universe governed by a Supreme Being with a moral purpose. In the latter alternative we introduce the element of morality as carried in the concept of a God and His purpose. Accord with that God and purpose is defined as moral; opposition is considered immoral.

With life God gave man freedom, and placed a world at his disposal. Man may choose to accept God or deny Him, he may recognize or ignore the laws that govern the universe, but, no matter what his choice, the laws remain unchanged. They operate for those who deny as well as for those who accept; the rain falls on the just and on the unjust, and the sun shines on the wicked as well as on the Godly. It is in man and not in the laws that we find morality or immorality.

There is harmony in the universe. The infinite number and variety of parts of which it is constituted must articulate and coordinate or the whole would fall apart. The same harmony must exist among the laws that govern the universe. Among them are laws that apply to all fields of activity and relationship, including a number which are of particular importance in the coordination of religion and economics.

11

Basic to both, these laws afford a foundation on which can be reared a structure of behavior consistent with both.

a. *The Law of Cause and Effect:*

The Will of God is primal cause. The universe and its operation are the effect of that Cause. We are not the helpless victims of irresponsible and mischievous spirits or demons, nor of blind materialistic forces, or sheer mathematical accident. The infinite care with which the relations of the spheres have been worked out is evidence of a supreme intelligence which valued order and dependable regularity above the chaos out of which they came. Such order and regularity continuing are evidence of cause and effect at work in the universe. It is not mere accident, for example, that the astronomer can measure the movements of the spheres and predict within seconds the time that a heavenly body will cross a designated spot, even though a thousand years elapse between the crossings.

Laws that govern the relationship of bodies in the universe and the life that is on them, are the implemented will of the supreme intelligence that created and rules them. Man cannot create laws of life, nor change them after God has set them in motion. And it is the part of wisdom to understand those laws and adapt our lives to them.

It is the essence of the law of cause and effect that once a cause is initiated or set in motion, the appropriate effect automatically follows. What that effect will be depends upon the nature of the circumstances, the act or event and the conditions under which it is set in motion, but the effect follows inexorably. As revealed in the laws of physics with its resultant motions from a combination of forces acting at the same time and in different directions, so the effect that would automatically follow a cause can be modified by immediately setting in motion other causes which would work as do the forces in physics and produce a composite or resultant effect. This resultant effect might differ much or little from the effect that was due to follow the original cause in that situation, depending upon the time of incidence and the relative force of the causes at work. However, also as in physics, if the causes or forces were not simultaneous or so close in time as to be practically simultaneous, we would likely have a series or sequence of effects whose order would depend upon the varying lag between cause and effect in each of the combinations involved. Each of the effects would act as a new cause in combination with other effects as they followed, and in turn bring still other effects.

It is because of the law of cause and effect that the individual human being can acquire dominion over other creatures and finally subdue the earth. In the meantime that individual is continually modifying his situations or creating new situations within the limits of his power to understand and act, by setting in motion the series of causes that he believes will bring the results desired. It is thus that the law is also the basis of all planning for the future. The great difficulty is in separating out the desired causes and avoiding consequent and subsequent effects that would act as causes to bring unanticipated and even undesired effects. The problem is to select accurately the factors chosen as causes and to discern in advance their movement and effect through the maze of complicated event, circumstance and condition which follow.

It is important to understand that cause and effect do not take into account the motives that initiate the acts which set the law in motion. Good motives do not modify results, and are futile unless intelligently applied in setting causes in motion.

The universality and immutability of the law of cause and effect is God's way of being omnipresent and omnipotent. We know Him by His works.

b. *The Law of Self-Preservation:*

This is the most basic of the laws that govern the life of a human being. It is rooted in the source of all human activity, the instinct of self-preservation. In its simplest and most crude forms this instinct has to do with sheer animal needs essential to continued existence. But, even with the refinements that result from experience, education and culture, the basic instinct is the same. Its expressions become refined, but the root is still the instinct that God implanted in man when He created him.

In terms of relations with his fellow-man this instinct in man becomes the motive of self-interest. It is the motivation of man's efforts to acquire and defend possessions, to increase quantity and improve their quality. When lifting intelligence enables man to sense the importance of his soul and a life hereafter, the same basic instinct motivates his actions toward the higher and nobler accomplishment.

It can truthfully be said that the development of personality, the realization of man's possibilities and his growth toward oneness with God, stem from this instinct of self-preservation. That apparently was God's way of motivating man toward achievement of his ultimate destiny. He did not leave it to chance, but implanted the instinct in man with all the force of a law, compelling, certainly impelling, the individual to exercise his will and freedom of choice in preservation of himself from loss, denial or destruction.

While the remaining laws enumerated in this chapter are shown as coordinate with the law of self-preservation, the reader is asked to keep in mind that all of them grow out of this basic law and the instinct which is its root.

c. *The Law of Wants:*

In using whatever means necessary to his existence, preservation and development, man engages in the process of satisfying his wants. The quantity and quality of those wants are a measure of the development of man and the life he lives.

Behind the wants, and expressing itself through them, is the never-ceasing urge of the instinct of self-preservation. Therefore, wants are insatiable. There is no limit to the expansibility of man's wants within the length, breadth and depth of life itself. If, tonight, all the wants of any individual could be listed and provision made for immediate satisfying of them, you may be sure that on the morrow the imagination of man building on the experience of those satisfactions, would conceive new and additional wants still to be satisfied. That is why progress never ceases, even though we change its direction and tempo.

That is why, in economics, there can be no static society or fixed stability. In an ocean of inequalities and variable individual endowments, the urge of self-preservation becomes the ceaseless pressure of insatiable wants for change and development. Goals reached automatically become the vantage points from which vistas of new goals challenge and awaken new efforts and ambitions.

d. *The Law of Growth:*

Struggle is the essence of existence, and the way of growth. The expenditures of energy in discovery, adaptation and application, and the accretion of energy through development, all in the process of satisfying wants, these constitute growth.

To grow is to live. To cease growing is to die. To satisfy wants there must be expenditure of energy, but the energy expended must be equaled or exceeded by the potential energy taken in through want satisfaction. *Otherwise there can be no development and no growth.* When the intake of energy exceeds the output there is growth. Conversely, when the output exceeds the intake growth ceases and deterioration toward death begins.

Growth can only be out of a surplus of intake over expenditure resulting from struggle for existence. And man grows, thanks to the instinct of self-preservation that drives him to take in more than he expends in the process of acquisition.

Struggle is the essence of existence not only for the animal, and essential to persistence of the species, but it also becomes the essence of evolution from animal to man and from man to spirit. The individual human being in effect fights his way to God by mastering his animal instincts and desires to the end of moral and spiritual growth. And it is through mastery of himself, thus becoming the captain of his personal powers and resources, that the individual man gains dominion over other creatures and finally subdues the earth.

It is not a process of destroying the basic instinct that motivates and empowers the individual, but its more effective use. Thus, the same instinct of self-preservation finds expression in the more refined processes of living and provides the core of what is called the "profit motive." What we know as the ambitions of men, be they for material gain, power, fame, service or even sacrifice of self to nobler need, are rooted back in that basic instinct and are part of the ceaseless struggle which is the essence of existence, source of the accretion which sustains life and provides the surplus out of which comes growth.

It seems apparent that God decreed from the very beginning that man should live and grow by overcoming. Subduing the earth and gaining dominion over its creatures calls for mastery through incessant effort and struggle. Throughout nature, in the world of realities, we see manifest on every hand the same theme that runs from the beginning through the Book of books until, at the end of that Book, man is given one of the most glorious promises ever recorded: "He that overcometh shall inherit all things; and I will be his God, and he shall be my son." (Rev. 21, 7)

e. *The Law of Mutuality of Interest:*

This law has been well stated by one of the lesser philosophers,* who wrote: "The purpose of man is self-preservation and to lead a happy life. Experience teaches him that other people are necessary to him. It shows him how he can make them useful to his designs. He sees what is approved and what causes displeasure. Such experiences give him a notion of what is just. Virtue, like wickedness, is not founded on conventions but on relationships between the members of the human race. *The mutual obligations of men derive from their need of using means apposite to the objectives which their nature sets them. It is by contributing to the happiness of others that we bind them to contribute to ours.*" Thus the individual self-interest is promoted through recognition of mutual interest.

Whether we justify this mutuality, or greatest happiness for the greatest number, on the ground of self-interest to the individual or on the ground of the social needs of mankind, it still remains a basic law of life. It is the cementing element that holds the family together as the social unit which, in turn, is united with other families in the total social structure.

We must recognize that, when creating man, God provided for his continuing existence by implanting within him the instinct of self-preservation, flowering in individual initiative, as basic to all human activity.

The law applies to all living things and is especially evident in the lives of bees, ants and herds of animals. It is doubtful that the ant or bee depend on reasoning from cause to effect to discover that the best way to preserve individual self-interest is through protection of the group. The same can be said for the individual buffalo who took his place in the ring of bulls around their cows and calves when wolves attacked the herd. It is more than probable that the recognition of mutuality of interest by these and other living species is the action of pure instinct for self-preservation combining with memory of previous experience to protect the individuals through group action, necessitated by common danger or desire.

---

*Baron Paul Holbach: 1723-1789; French materialistic philosopher, hostile to religious teachings. It is interesting to note that even the materialistic philosopher must recognize mutuality of interest, though he phrase it somewhat differently than did Jesus of Nazareth.

Recognition of mutual interest is a refinement of the sheer instinct of self-preservation. In man that recognition was undoubtedly aided by reflection following perception through experience, whereas in lower species of creatures it was pure instinct and survival of the more fit that preserved those species which acted in accord with the law of mutuality of interest.

It is no less important for man to recognize the same law, as it was revealed to us by God through Jesus. So recognized, the natural law is lifted to the dignity of an ordinance of God. Because of this law, seeking his individual self-interest, man is impelled to live and work with other men and thereby strengthen their common effort to subdue the earth. God multiplies the effectiveness of the most basic urge implanted in man, the instinct of self-preservation, as the law of mutuality of interest impels coordination of human effort in the best interests of all men.

f. *The Law of Freedom Is the Law of Self-Control:*

Individual man is endowed by God with freedom. Stewardship must carry with it not only responsibility but the power to perform that stewardship voluntarily. There can be freedom only if the choice is voluntary.

But, "voluntary" does not mean absence of all restraint.

Long ago the physicist thought of a molecule of matter as the unit of being. Then he learned that the real unit is the atom within the molecule, or energy itself. He sought to split the atom, searching out the secret of its being. Years and years of research, and then—with one horrendous, heaven-torturing explosion, with the civilization-challenging destruction of an entire city and the thousands of human motes caught within its reach, he demonstrated the secret of economic, political and social organization.

Energy is life and life is energy. But, energy uncontrolled, running wild, is destructive of life. Its destructiveness is in direct ratio to the amount of energy imprisoned, the smallness of the space within which it is compressed, and the suddenness with which it is released. The atomic bomb is the most physically destructive thing the world has yet known because of the enormous energy compressed within the almost incomprehensibly small space.

The same energy that is so frightfully destructive can be made to work productively if it is harnessed and directed. All the universe is energy. Without a coordinating purpose that energy would waste itself in destruction of the very universe it constitutes. But the universe survives and moves on toward its destiny because it is held together by the Will of God implemented in the natural laws that coordinate and guide its energies. God harnessed the energy that holds the world within His will.

Man himself is energy, held in leash and utilized by automatic devices fashioned within the human body, plus the will by which man chooses what to do with the energy that is himself, as well as that available for his use. Even man destroys himself if his energies are not harnessed. Rightly directed by the individual himself, adapted to the natural laws by which God governs the universe, the will of man can become the most constructive force on earth. Running wild or organized in defiance of natural law, the human will can defeat the very purpose of God in man, for it is of God, unless God destroy the man before the man destroys God.

Out of discipline and direction of individual will grows the form and character of society, the social and economic structure which results from the relationships of man with God and with other men and the physical world in which they live.

There can be no "laissez-faire" in the sense of absence of restraints of man. The question for civilized man is whether the control over the energies of the individual shall be from within the man or from outside.

If the control of the individual is from within himself he is free. He may discipline himself severely and even remorselessly, deny his body gratification of its yearnings, and force himself to work until he drops from sheer exhaustion. But, so long as it is HIS will that gives commands to himself, voluntarily, he is free.

On the other hand, if the control or direction of the individual is from outside himself, he is not free. He may suffer little restraint, he may gratify his yearnings and work almost not at all, and yet be a slave, if the control come from outside himself. And it does not matter whether that outside control is exercised by individuals, associations of men or through the instrumentalities we call government, whether it be benign or hurtful in its aims and consequences, he is still not a free man.

The test holds even when the individual is employed by another person, and thus sells his services for wages or fees. If he does the work voluntarily in performance of a contract voluntarily entered, or because of sheer pride of craftsmanship, he is a free man. It is only when he is forced, when he works without voluntary direction of his own will, or ceases work involuntarily in response to forces outside him, that he loses the freedom God gave him.

It is energy released from within, voluntarily, that attains the greatest potential usefulness under direction of the human will. The highest order of social organization and progress grows out of voluntary organization and multiplication of the efforts of individual men and women. Organization can effect and maintain the highest welfare of man only as it is done through voluntary coordination of free individuals, each making his own choices within the limits of common purpose and in response to the law of mutuality of interest.

The law of freedom is the law of self-command. It is the will of the individual making choices for that individual and directing the energies of which the individual is constituted. Freedom lies in self-mastery, in triumph of the spiritual man over the material creature out of which he evolved. "He that ruleth his own spirit is greater than he that taketh a city."

g. *Man Cannot Live without Faith:*

Faith is as vital to being as are food and drink.

Knowledge is limited to experience. Beyond that we must depend upon faith supported by reason. Since we cannot, with our finite and limited minds, know and understand all, we must act on faith after sample experience has indicated what we may expect on subsequent trials. So long as faith continues to be justified by results we stick to it. We change our faith only when it no longer works.

It is so that faith becomes knowledge, lifting us progressively from level to higher level of understanding and mastery. The simplest acts, such as eating food which one has eaten before, can be performed only as we have faith. Without faith there cannot be sufficient certainty to risk the act. Even that which we understand is of no avail without faith, for faith is needed to believe even that which we already understand. We cannot know, even upon repetition, that similar causes will be followed by similar effects until after experience has demonstrated whether we were right or wrong. Therefore, faith is preliminary to action even when it is in a reality we already understand.

It is unfortunate that education has led men to insist on understanding as preliminary to faith. Followed logically, that would make one refuse to use an electrical device unless he first could be shown exactly what electricity is. He would deny the existence of the atom because he never saw one and did not understand just how it functioned. No one refuses to avail himself of a service because he does not understand just how it is performed.

Some truths can be demonstrated, but the highest truths often escape demonstration, since they lie outside the borders of human experience. For them we must rely on faith, supported by reason. Even faith cannot convince us of anything that contradicts our knowledge, unless it is supported by reason.

The one faith that has never failed us is faith in Providence, in a God of Purpose whose laws rule the universe and govern all life. We cannot measure God nor test Him. We accept Him or reject Him, but we cannot ignore Him and live. It is the function of experience to test faith and the results of faith, of reason to support the projection of faith into acts not yet tested by experience, and none of these can happen without faith. Without faith man could not act in the present nor plan for the future. It was a great apostle who told us: "Now faith is the substance of things hoped for, the evidence of things not seen." And Paul knew.

To avoid confusion we should distinguish between the "Laws of God" discussed in the previous chapter and the "Laws of Life" discussed in this chapter.

Both sets of laws are manifestations of the Will of God. The "Laws of Life" or natural laws, also called "principles of nature," once set in motion act automatically and require no reflection to make them function, without regard for motives or morals. They apply to animals as such, along with all other living things, and are God's way of preserving life in organic matter.

The "Laws of God," including the Ten Commandments and the Golden Rule, are special ordinances of God, given to man as rules for his conduct in relation to God and man, and the stewardship vested in him.

While the "Laws of Life" or natural laws are principles which automatically govern creatures without volition of the creature, the "Laws of God" are ordinances which man can either accept or reject, obey or disregard as the rules of conduct in his personal relations to God, family and society. They are the adequately comprehensive admonitions from which can be built sound individual, family and social life, at the volition of the individual human being.

The natural laws relate creature to creature as the material product of automatic principles. The ordinances of God become the basis of religious observance and voluntary obedience to the will of God. There is no conflict between the two sets of laws. They supplement each other and enable man to continue his moral and spiritual evolution out of his existence as a creature.

CHAPTER 3

TWO GREAT CHOICES

BECAUSE man cannot live without faith, the freedom God gave him must begin with what he chooses to believe. If that choice is denied him he loses freedom itself. Our subsequent choices and actions are finally the result of what we believe. The policies pursued and courses of action taken may have their roots in time and space far afield from the areas in which they take effect, but their beginnings are no less surely in the basic assumptions from which we take our faith.

The application of faith to fact involves two very important choices. On the nature of the decisions made depends whether we find the faith of religion and the facts of economics in harmony or in conflict.

THE FIRST CHOICE: MORAL PURPOSE OR BLIND FORCE

We must choose between a universe guided by moral purpose and governed by laws designed to effect that purpose, and, on the other hand, a universe ruled by blind forces and mathematical chance, without moral purpose or spiritual guidance.

In terms of personalities, it is such a choice as one would make between Jesus of Nazareth and Karl Marx of Germany.

We are free to commit our faith to either concept and proceed accordingly. But, once we have chosen, either deliberately or by default, we are committed to either a spiritual or a materialistic approach to the situations of which we are part.

If we chose to believe in God and a moral purpose in the universe, we would be bound to accept the laws of God in fulfilling that purpose, to adapt our lives to those laws as we became aware of them. He who believes in the freedom and dignity of the individual, responsible to God for that freedom and dignity, must also accept this alternative. Conversely, he who accepts the alternative of faith in God must also believe in the freedom and dignity of the individual, responsible as an individual to God. Even the government, or the state, must recognize itself as responsible to God and subordinate its interests as a state to the inherent rights of the individual human being.

It is in recognition of the paramountcy of the individual human being that our United States Constitution includes the Bill of Rights, and guarantees those rights to even one lone individual against the entire federal government and the majority of the people themselves. That is what makes it possible for us to remain free.

If we accept the belief that the universe is without moral purpose or supreme God Who has implemented that purpose with natural law, we are bound to accept the control of man by the state, for then the individual is not longer master by virtue of rights inherent in him from his Creator. He must look instead to those who control the state for such rights and measure of individual freedom as they deign to permit him. Conversely, those who recognize the state as paramount, as the source of rights and well-being for the individual, must deny the existence of rights inherent in the individual and the responsibility of that individual to God as laid down in the First Commandment.

THE SECOND CHOICE: APPROACH TO IMPROVEMENT

We must choose the approach and method to improve the economic status of all men, particularly the great mass of humanity who live close to the level of mere subsistence in many parts of the world today. This choice extends also to the social and political status of man, for we cannot separate economic freedom from the other freedoms. We have two alternatives.

The first alternative is the outgrowth of a widely-accepted school of thought which considers the mass of individuals unfit for or incapable of self-government, and has little or no faith in the ability or disposition of individuals to make wise choices in the determination of their affairs. This school of thought holds that systems control and shape men, and that individuals can be improved and their status raised only by first changing the systems under which they live. Hence, there follows the necessity of control by government, with sufficient power to change the economic system which determines the individual's status.

The other alternative is to attack the problem through the individual. Here the assumption is that systems grow out of the character and relations of men, rather than the systems determining the character and relations of men. Those who accept this approach emphasize the individual as basic to government, rather than government as essential to the individual. They would improve men and be rewarded with improved institutions in consequence. They hold the individual responsible to God for his stewardship and would have society depend upon better men rather than more laws or a powerful central state, for the good of all.

The choices must be made in pairs. If we have faith in God and moral purpose we are also logically under necessity of seeking the betterment of society through improvement and voluntary coordination of individuals. If we choose to believe in blind force and a material universe without moral purpose, we must no less surely depend upon the power of the state to plan and provide for its individual subjects.

The choice may be made by default, through accepting what seems an inevitable current trend. It has been pointed out that in earlier days we developed customs out of commonly accepted practices, that those customs constituted our social controls, and even the sanction for statutory law. Statutory laws could not survive unless they were in accord with custom. This was illustrated by the failure of the Eighteenth Amendment to the Constitution.

But, we are also told, in later years the tempo of social change has increased so rapidly that customs no longer develop in time to regulate the new situations and conditions. So, instead of waiting for customs to develop, and then base statutory laws on established custom, we find it necessary to meet the changed conditions with immediate statutory regulations, thus reversing the process and developing custom out of statutory law instead of long continued practices.

The terrible significance of that change is apparently missed by those who complacently accept the change. They fail to see the most important consequence of the reversal of the process. When custom is developed, as normally, out of oft-repeated and common practices, approving the practices as proper, it grows really out of the choices that determine the acts which in turn establish the custom. Behind every act is a choice, whether or not the person acting is aware of the fact. And every choice is based on the religion or personal code of conduct of the individual. So the full sequence begins with religion, or nature of the Deity accepted as final arbiter and judge of conduct. Then come the choices which result in acts, which in turn develop into custom and finally flower in statutory law. But the base and root of that structure of sequence is faith in and worship of the Deity.

Reversing the process, we begin with statutory law, grown out of the ideas and standards of those persons in control of government, and chosen to fit a particular situation or purpose of those in control. Then we proceed from the law to establish custom through enforced acceptance and obedience to the law. In turn, the statutorily-established custom now makes the individual act in accord with the custom, thus determining our choices, out of necessity, from law; and to the extent that our individual codes of conduct, or religion, conflict with those choices, we must adjust those codes of conduct or religion to the "practical world" established by statutory law. In a sentence, the reversal of the process leads toward the ultimate substitution of the State for God as the final arbiter and judge of our conduct. And, regardless of Whom or What we *profess* to worship, our real god is whomever or whatever we accept as the arbiter of what is right or wrong, good or bad. *That is the ultimate significance of seeking betterment for society through the state rather than through voluntary improvement of the individual.*

There is no more significant illustration of this point than the work and teachings of Jesus of Nazareth. He made the individual the beginning and end of His ministry. It is enormously significant that Jesus, Son of God, bringing man the vital truths he needed to meet the problems of his day and for the future, did not set aside ancient truths in attempting to establish any new political or economic system. He could have made Himself master of the then known world, but, instead, He poured out His life in a small corner of that world in an effort to change the thinking of individual men and women and to induce them to accept individual responsibility to God for the betterment of their lives. He brought a doctrine which would change the entire world, once it was adopted as the rule for living by individual man. He knew that if men, as individuals, made themselves fit for freedom and self-government, the ills of the worst system would pass away. And He knew also that, unless men did change themselves, any system would permit them to become slaves to their own appetites or to other men. *His answer was not more governmnt laws or mere change in form of government. His answer was BETTER MEN.*

And it is this answer in widely accepted Christian principles, that would either make unnecessary any substitution of statutory law for custom as means to meet rapidly-changing conditions or situations, or would provide the actual code or religious base on which even emergency legislation could be drawn and erected.

It seems clear to the author that the school of thought exemplified by Jesus has brought far greater and more wide-spread progress to the world than has any other school of thought, especially that of Karl Marx. There can be no doubt as to which of the alternatives seems best to the author. However, it is a question for the reader to determine for himself, whether or not he truly believes in individual freedom and responsibility. For it is largely on that premise that the choice will be made.

PART TWO—ECONOMICS

(As Discovered in a Study of Fact)

Economics has to do with the activities and resulting relationships and institutions of man, which arise out of his efforts to make a living.

Chapter 1

INTRODUCTION

W E must deal with the facts of economics before we can adopt any sensible policy with respect to situations which have arisen out of them. Therefore, this second part of the book is devoted to those facts.

It is obviously impossible to make the second part of this book sufficiently complete to give the entire economic picture. Special fields, further subdivisions of those considered, cannot be included because of the physical limitations. But the author has endeavored to describe the most basic of the economic facts, especially those which are often and hurtfully misunderstood or mistakenly presented or used. The material here developed should be helpful to those who would understand economics and its practical correlations in religion.

When the reader comes to make his own conclusions and deductions, he is urged never to forget that any answer reached may not safely ignore the facts. No student of economics dare ignore the law of self-preservation or the instinct in which it is rooted. He must remember that goods can come only out of the application of human effort to natural resources and that we must produce more before we can have more.

These are not special pleadings: they are unbiased actual fact. To ignore them is as unwise as it would be for an engineer to ignore the law of gravity.

The taproot of all economics is human wants. All we know in economics and as economics is the result of our efforts to satisfy human wants. Because these wants are insatiable, and because Providence has not provided all that man wants in the form, time and place in which he wants it, it is necessary for man, in "the sweat of his face," to produce the goods himself, through his own efforts. That is production.

Out of production, or necessitated by it, arise all the processes of economics beginning with exchange and going on to their common progeny of distribution, money and all the rest. So our study of fact begins properly with the study of production.

29

CHAPTER 2

PRODUCTION

PRODUCTION is the creation of utility with which to satisfy human wants. The utility may consist of or be in material goods or human services.

a. *The Genesis of Production:*

In the world which evolved out of chaos were all the materials and forces that are in the world today. But they did not exist or were not available in the form that they are today. The treasures of earth were there, but they were hidden and had to be discovered. The materials and forces which are so commonplace today were mysteries then, waiting to be pierced and developed.

Into that world came man. He wanted things then as he does today, in order to live. And then, as today, those things which he used to satisfy his wants possessed utility, or the ability to satisfy wants. In other words, they were useful to him because they satisfied his wants. And the better they could satisfy his wants, the more useful they were. Thus, the essential quality of goods was their utility. That is true today.

The things which man needs and desires to satisfy his wants did not then, nor do not today, lie at hand waiting to be appropriated and used by man. There was some usefulness in the materials which man found at hand in the beginnings, but not as much as he wanted, and so, to natural resources man had to add human energy to make things already existing more useful to himself.

He had to struggle, to expend energy, if he would exist.

30

The process of man working with nature, digging out her gifts, piercing her mysteries and changing things to make them more useful, that is production. *Production is the application of human energy to natural resources to make those resources more useful to man.*

b. *Primitive Man:*

Life was simple, scant and precarious for the primitive man. He had only what he could take with his bare hands and all of his time was consumed in eking out a bare existence. Because of the urge that drives man ceaselessly, primitive man was not satisfied. He wanted more goods, more to eat, more to wear and enjoy as comforts against the elements with which he had constantly to struggle.

He discovered that his muscle power was limited. Using it he had improved his conditions by making available natural resources more useful to him, but he soon reached the limits of that power. He learned that if he was to have more goods he must find a way to make that limited muscle power more effective, to produce more goods per unit of time and energy.

Through his crude discoveries and experiments he learned the division of labor, he invented tools, and out of these, with their continuously increasing effectiveness, there grew ultimately the thing we call civilization.

c. *Division of Work:*

Perhaps the earliest way man found to make his work more effective was to discover aptitudes for certain kinds of work and for an individual to specialize on one kind of activity while others specialized on other kinds of activity. The same principle was found effective within activities as men found it worth while to split the total process of making something into parts, and assigning some men to perform some parts while other men performed other parts of the total task. As they developed greater skill by virtue of repetition of aptitude, a given amount of energy and time could result in more creation of utility.

Two primitive men, hunting and fishing side by side, discovered that one of them was the better fisherman, and that the other was the more expert hunter. They agreed to specialize. One would do all the fishing and the other would do all the hunting. Thus, without increasing the amount of effort expended, or the time over which to expend it, they increased the number of fish and rabbits which they caught. Their work had become more effective and they had more to eat.

They also had a new problem, for after they specialized, one of them had all the fish and the other had all the rabbits. If each was to have a combination of both kinds of food it would be necessary to exchange fish for rabbits. And there emerged the granddaddy of all economic problems: how much of each for the other. But that is a problem for later discussion.

Even while the process of division and specialization of work was going on, it was already apparent that time was still limited, and, even with the greater muscle power utilization, new limits of production would soon be reached. Wants continued to expand, existing methods of getting goods still lacked the power of satisfying all the wants, and man began his search for tools.

d. *Tools and Harnessing Natural Forces:*

Primitive man discovered that a rock was more effective than his bare fist in cracking nuts or in crushing the head of an animal. The same rock, fastened with fibers to the end of a stick, could be swung with still greater force, and man had discovered the hammer.

An edge chipped on the piece of rock made it into an ax, and man had a cutting tool.

Fibers interlaced made a surface which could catch objects larger than the spaces between the fibers while letting smaller objects or fluids through. It was as though man had much enlarged his hands, and increased his effectiveness in using the net in catching fish out of the shallows of streams. Later he found ways of using the net in deeper waters.

The bow and arrow saved running up to the rabbit to catch it. A trap for rabbits used the energy of the rabbit itself with the strength of bent saplings to catch the rabbits in still greater numbers.

Man had added the use of a natural force to apply in place of his own energy to the tool, through which he had already increased the effectiveness of his own energy. The next step was machines to harness and use the forces of nature for the production of goods.

So, with one step after another, man used his own muscle power to harness and direct other powers which he found available for the driving of his tools. Wind, gravity, steam, electricity, the internal combustion of fuel, and soon-to-come atomic energy, have almost completely supplanted the muscle power with which man once had to do his work.

As a savage with his bare hands man had a productive capacity of about one tenth of one horsepower. Today, with the wealth and intricate development of tools, machinery, technological processes and mechanical power, man has an average productive capacity in the United States of about ten horsepower. He is able to produce about one hundred times as much in the same time, and with less effort, as could his primitive ancestor.

e. *Factors in Production:*

NATURAL RESOURCES

The foundation factor in production is nature or "natural resources," the materials and forces provided as part of the world in which we live.

WORK OR "LABOR"

Man found it necessary to add his own energy to natural resources to make them useful in satisfying his wants. Thus he created utility with the second factor in production, work or "labor." This factor can create utility either by changing already existing materials so as to make them more useful, or by performing some act which directly satisfies a want. The first is illustrated by weaving fibers into a loin cloth, which increases the utility of the fibers: the second is seen in fetching the fibers for the person who wants to weave them into a cloth. The baking of bread is production by making grain more useful; and the shampooing of a lady's hair in a beauty parlor is a direct satisfaction of the want, or a personal service.

TOOLS OR "CAPITAL"

Tools and machinery and the accessories necessary to procure and use them, constitute the third factor in production, collectively and traditionally known as "capital." "Capital" is the child of natural resources and work. In this broad sense we can use interchangeably the term "tools."

RISK TAKER

All tools and machinery are the result of past savings as well as of work. In producing them someone had to forego immediate satisfaction of some of his wants and take the risk of getting or not getting a return later on. So we have a fourth factor in production who is the *risk taker,* often called the "enterpriser" or "entrepreneur." He is very important and deserves special consideration. Whatever be his income, it results from the productivity of the tools he owns, their efficiency in making human energy more effective in creating utility, the ability of goods to satisfy wants. The risk taker also may be the worker, thus combining two productive functions in one person.

f. *Management for Effective Utilization:*

"Natural Resources," combined with human energy (work or "labor") and tools and machinery ("capital"), cannot reach their greatest effectiveness until they are properly adapted, combined and directed. That requires initiative, enterprise, organization and supervision, in short, management. The human resources of any country are its most precious asset. And the important task of any country is to secure maximum utilization of its human resources, human energy at work on the materials of nature.

Management itself is an important part of our human resources. Early in the history of civilization there arose individuals with more initiative and resourcefulness than their fellows. They conceived projects to be performed; new things to make, better ways of making things already known; they saved out of their incomes through self-denial or borrowed the savings of others who had not consumed all their income, then invested or risked those savings in financing their projects. They furnished the tools made available from the savings they had themselves accumulated or had borrowed, and undertook to pay other human beings for helping them to carry out their projects. The economist has designated these individuals by the French term, "Entrepreneur," meaning enterprisers or risk takers.

So the classic economists (Adam Smith and his followers) came to name four factors in production: nature, labor, capital and the entrepreneur.

The functions of the entrepreneur or risk taker included saving, investing, risk-taking, organization, planning and supervision, all that is involved in initiating and running an enterprise as well as furnishing the tools and machinery. Frequently even today both functions of investing and managing are combined in one person, especially in small business. But there has grown up a great class of individuals, really a special classification of "labor," who specialize in management, undertaking the initiating of an enterprise, or taking over one already under way, and even using some of their own capital or savings, but securing much if not most and sometimes all of the funds needed, from other persons.

The risk-takers in the modern corporate form of business may become either bond-holders or stock-holders. The bond-holders loan money to a business and are creditors. The stock-holders own shares in the business and elect the directors. But both of them are investors and furnish the means with which to buy the tools, machinery and other essentials with which to run the business. Employed management runs the business subject to the approval of the stock-holders, acting through their Board of Directors.

Because of its effectiveness in combining the other factors in production, and thereby securing a greater amount and better quality of product (more total utility) than could otherwise be secured, management is undoubtedly the most productive of all the factors in production. Modern industry and a high degree of civilization growing out of the division of labor and the use of tools, would be impossible without management.

Wherever we find individuals free and protected in their rights to enter into contract, to initiate enterprise, to work as hard and long as they wish, and to compete with each other, we are likely to find the most efficient management. That is because there is real incentive for effort and because management under such conditions is not limited to certain classes of the population or chosen by government. Instead it is selected as to fitness through a process of competition.

Our management is drawn from all classes of the population, from poorest to richest, and is chosen for its efficiency in making human effort in the person of the worker more productive with the tools and machinery furnished him. This efficiency is demonstrated in the process of business, and the process of selection follows the teachings in the famous parable of the talents. He that is faithful in few things is recognized and is placed over many things.

That is why the United States, already providing workers with more and better tools, develops the most efficient management and has the most productive economy in the world. That is why we have the highest real wages, best values for the consumer and a profit for the investor, in spite of substantial deductions through government exactions called taxes.

g. *What We Produce:*

Man does not create in the sense that he adds to the mass of material or volume of energy in the world. There is no change in either. As it was in the beginning so is the total mass of matter and volume of energy now and will be. Man does not create either.

What man does is to make existing things more useful to himself, harness natural energy to make it work for him and add to the utility with which to satisfy his wants. What man actually creates is some quality which makes things more useful than they were. He creates ability to satisfy wants, in one word, *he creates utility.*

He does this in four ways.

Form utility. We can make things more useful by changing their form, or combining them in new and different forms, in consequence of which things have greater ability to satisfy wants. So, each of the thousands of parts which finally constitute an automobile has a certain amount of utility. But, by combining them into an automobile, tires, spark plugs, steering gears, and all the rest, we get a resultant utility which is greater than the sum total of the utility of the various parts, each by itself. That is production. Sewing cotton cloth, after the cotton has been made into cloth, gives you the same cotton, less the portion lost in trimming, but the utility of the dress, *as* a dress, is greater than that of the total cotton used in the making, as cotton or as cloth.

Place utility. Ice in April has little usefulness in northern Canada. Any one ton of ice up there could be spared without ever missing it because the people up there have more than they need. But, in the warm climate of New Orleans, that ton of ice would be very useful in making and keeping things cool. Anyone who moved that ton of ice from northern Canada to New Orleans would be creating utility, place utility, because he would be moving the ice from a place where it had no utility to another place where it had great utility.

Time utility. We have an abundance of food at harvest time each year, more than we can then eat; and any one unit of food then has so little usefulness that it could be destroyed without denying the satisfaction of a single want. But through the months before the next harvest comes, the supply of food would spoil unless some way were found to preserve it. And those who preserve that food from the time when it has little utility until the later time when it has great utility, thereby add to its utility or usefulness in satisfying important wants which would otherwise have to go unsatisfied. Thus, utility is created by keeping a good from one time when it is not needed until a later time when it is needed, or when the need is greater than it was before the article was preserved.

Personal Services. There are some wants that can be satisfied only through the direct use of human energy. Thus, a man wants his hair cut and cannot well cut it himself. The barber who cuts his hair for him is rendering a personal service, and thereby satisfying a human want. He is a producer. We can even think of this barber as adding to the usefulness of the man if the latter, for example, happens to be an actor the appearance of whose hair is important to his success in acting. The barber has increased the ability of the actor to render his service to the audience. The actor is more efficient in his role than he would otherwise be.

So with the services of the doctor, dentist, lawyer, and the host of others who serve their fellow-men. All of them are producers.

The clerks in an office, the boy who operates an elevator, the street sweeper, the taxi-driver and all the almost infinite variety of those who render personal service or aid to those who in turn actually change the form, place or time of things, are all producers.

In brief, anyone who in any way renders a service or performs an act directly helpful or that is even remotely essential or helpful to the process of actual production of utility, is himself a producer. No good is finally produced until it is in the hands of the consumer, ready for the satisfaction of a human want.

h. *The Place of Profit in Production:*

As already shown, the productiveness of management is not due to the greater expenditure of human energy by workers under the supervision of management. Instead, it is due to the greater utilization of the energy and multiplication of its results. The multiplication is accomplished through the use of tools, division of work, adaptation of special skills, and use of mechanical power through machinery, all of which, effectively combined and supervised, make each unit of human energy more productive than it could otherwise be. Not only has management NOT made its contribution to increased production by exacting more energy from workers, but has actually contrived to get more production with less physical expenditure of energy than was necessary before management became so effective.

Out of the multiplied effectiveness of human energy applied to natural resources has grown what we know as civilization, with all the material and non-material evidences that constitute and demonstrate that civilization.

But all of these evidences go back to a simple fact which is often overlooked in its most important function, a fact which can fairly be called the "genesis of civilization." *That is profit.*

All improvement and progress in the life of man can be traced back to its beginnings in a surplus, something left over when the cost of actual living, or expenditure of energy necessary to sustain life has been met. That surplus is actually a profit, an excess of income over outgo. It is something that is left over when the expense of living has been met, a residue after immediate needs have been provided for.

For example: this surplus or profit may have consisted, long ago, of food enough to keep the man alive another day. He could have eaten all the food immediately and relied on his efforts of the next day to provide him with food for that day. But, instead, he denied himself the immediate additional gratification and saved the food. Thus, he saved his profit, or surplus. That made it possible for him to spend the entire next day working on an idea that had come to him. He wanted to make a stone hammer with which he could strike a harder blow, and more effective, than with his bare fist.

So he spent the next day in making a stone hammer instead of having to look for food, and subsisted instead on the food which was his surplus of yesterday. When the day was done he had his hammer, a tool with which he could multiply the effectiveness of his fist and arm. And, although he was hungry when the day ended he was able thereafter to accomplish more in any day than he had before, thus making possible still more production and a still greater surplus or profit.

Instead of making a hammer, he might have made a net to catch fish, or a trap to catch rabbits, or a plow to cultivate his land. In each case he would have turned his surplus or profit of one day into greater productive capacity on the next day.

So began the cycle: a surplus or profit, the saving of some of that surplus, the fashioning of the surplus into a tool or using the time so gained to make the tool, multiplied effectiveness of human energy, still greater productivity, higher standard of living and greater surplus along with it, still more saving, and so on around the cycle, ever and ever again.

The mite of original crude profit, a surplus of income over outgo or expenditures, multiplied over the centuries has given us accumulated capital goods with all the consequences of those goods, roads, factories, churches, schools, homes, automobiles, wash machines, books, instruments of all kinds and the whole myriad of things that have swelled into the far extent and mighty refinements of modern civilization. Without profit there would have been no tools, without tools no civilization!

i. *Summary:*

What the scientist calls evolution began with bringing order out of chaos and setting in motion the unending forces and energies through which materials pass in the cycles of their being. To these were added man, endowed with imagination, a measure of creative genius, and blessed with the goad of necessity. To his own personal qualities and power man has added tools, machines and technologies for developing the most effective methods and means to utilize the materials and forces of nature.

Through these man has changed the form of things, as in smelting iron out of ore and fashioning it into watch springs and other articles useful to man. He has changed the place of things, as in bringing oranges grown in Florida or California or Texas to many other places where oranges are desired but not available. He has changed the time of use of things, as in storing eggs from a time when they are plentiful and therefore of less individual use and value, to other times when they are not plentiful and therefore of greater use and value.

And he has rendered personal services, such as those of the dentist, the doctor, lawyer, house-servant, the barber and a host of others who minister to the needs of man by satisfying certain direct personal wants. Through all of these he has added utility to things, making them more useful, and even adding to the usefulness of persons, thereby creating utility or ability to satisfy wants. And the process is called production.

But it is in the development of man himself, the savage to civilized citizen, lifting himself through the centuries from the savage with bare hands to the use of tools, machinery and technology, and finally to management in discovering, selecting, segregating, combining, directing and supervising, that the individual demonstrates the creative power through which endowment and necessity brought civilization into being.

Basic to all economics is the fundamental truth that production is the source of all wealth and well-being through the satisfying of wants. Men and nations live and grow strong as they produce more. They weaken and ultimately die as they produce less. We can have more and be stronger only as we produce more per unit of time and energy, and employ enough of both time and energy to meet our needs. The alternative is to have less and be less than we now have and are.

CHAPTER 3

EXCHANGE

EXCHANGE is the process by which one person gives possession of some economic good to some other person in consideration of receiving possession of an economic good from that other person.

a. *The Genesis of Exchange:*

Out of the division of work came the real impetus that made man a social being. He had already known the need of combining efforts, standing together with his fellows when attacked by wild animals, or when he attempted tasks too great for the strength of one man. But division of work made additional demands and offered opportunities which the individual could meet only as a continuing member of society.

In consequence of division of work, and the specialization that necessarily went with it, one person had a surplus of one article or part while another person had a surplus of some other article or part. The only way that each could benefit from his own specialization was to exchange the products he had in surplus for some of the products that others had in surplus.

Production could not have developed beyond the most primitive level and would not today maintain its high level and full significance, were it not for the active functioning of exchange. On the other hand, without production there would be nothing to exchange. So these two basic and parent activities to all the rest of economics are mutually and inescapably dependent on each other. Each requires and rewards the other. This often over-looked fact has vital consequences in the relationships that develop among human beings and on the policies they determine for their individual and common improvement.

The original exchange was simple. For example, a fisherman who did nothing but fish and had more fish than he needed for his own consumption, exchanged some of his fish directly for the rabbits of a hunter who had caught more rabbits than he needed for his own consumption. Both, in turn, exchanged some of their fish and rabbits for the surplus carrots of a third person who wanted fish and rabbits to eat with his carrots. *This was called barter.*

The weakness of this kind of exchange, limiting the volume of goods that could be exchanged, lay in the fact that each party to the exchange had to find someone who had what he wanted and wanted what he had. That finally led to money, or the use of a third commodity or tool to serve as a go-between in the transaction.

It is a far cry from the open air trade of a rabbit for some fish or some carrots, to the elegantly appointed women's shop where a dress or some perfume is sold for money. The woman who buys the dress or the perfume probably does not have the ghost of an idea of where the dress or perfume came from or who made either, and yet the real exchange is the services of her husband in earning the money which she spends for the services of the person who made the dress or the perfume or contributed in any way to making the dress and perfume available to the woman who bought them.

How much of the services or efforts of one man, the husband, shall be given in payment for the services of another who makes the dress or perfume, constitutes the parent of most of the problems in economics. Among free men the decision is made by a process of bargaining: in a tyranny or dictatorship it is determined or regulated by directive from the government or ruling power.

But that is a problem to be attacked under the discussion of distribution, or division of the common product among those who pro-- duce it and determination of the relative shares of income for the individuals out of the total income of all.

The key to our problem of determining the ratios of exchange lies in the nature and motivation of the exchange itself.

b. *The Miracle of Exchange:*

What makes the exchange, or trade, possible is the fact that each party to the transaction wants something he does not have or of which he has less than he wants, and wants it more than he does something else which he already has or of which he has more than he wants. Therefore, he is willing to trade what he has for what he wants.

It is the Miracle of Exchange that both parties to the transaction make a profit or benefit by trading with each other. Without this miracle there would be no exchange.

It is on this same broad principle that we choose one occupation rather than another, forego one gratification and seek some other. It is rooted in the very instinct of self-preservation and is as inseparable from man as are the biological processes by which he is conceived, born and developed into an adult being. THE MARVEL OF MUTUALLY PROFITABLE EXCHANGE IS THE FOUNDATION ON WHICH WE BUILD INDIVIDUAL AND SOCIAL PROGRESS AND ALL THAT COOPERATION AMONG MEN MAKES POSSIBLE.

c. Motivation in Exchange:

Whatever motivates exchange is indispensable to any civilization which is based on the production and exchange of goods and services, which in turn result from increasingly effective utilization of human energy applied to natural resources. Out of such production and exchange comes the magnificent panorama of factories, churches, schools, roads, bridges, houses, banks, railroads, airplanes, wash machines, radios, and the myriad of devices and improvements that raise and maintain life above the level of subsistence.

The desire to benefit is the motivation to exchange.

This desire has also been called the acquisitive spirit or the profit motive. It does not matter what form the benefit may take, whether that of money, fame, power, peace, happiness, material goods, sacrifice for others or eternal bliss in heaven, so long as anyone is actuated by or sees some benefit in the exchange. In giving up one thing for some other which is more greatly desired by him than that which he gives up, the individual is actuated by the profit motive.

Profit is one of the most widely used and thoroughly misunderstood and abused terms in the entire language of economics. The same is true of the term and concept called the "profit motive." Because so many people, even good people, have been misinformed or emotionally misled, the very term "profit motive" connotes avarice and serves as a red flag to arouse their indignation as against something unjust and un-Christian, the very root of all evil and suffering.

Out of that misinformation and misunderstanding comes one of the most widely accepted errors in economic thinking, namely, the theory that we should have *production for use and not for profit.*

Correctly understood, there is and need be no conflict between the ideas of service or use and benefit or profit in the production of goods.

The *purpose* of production is to satisfy wants, or *use.* It dare not be anything else. No one could long stay in business unless he *did* produce for use. But the *motive or urge to which we must appeal in order to get production for use, is the profit motive,* the desire to benefit or profit in an exchange transaction.

If the producer is successful in producing for use, people will buy what he produces, and if he is efficient in producing it, he will be rewarded with a profit. If he is not successful in producing for use, makes something that people do not want, or is so inefficient that he makes it at too high cost and has to charge too much, people will not buy what he produces and he will suffer a loss.

Thus, hope and fear, basic human emotions, are reached through rewarding with profit and punishing with loss. *The hope for profit and fear of loss impels producers to make for use.* Thus, the *purpose of production is use,* while *the incentive* to produce for use *is the profit motive.*

It is as sound to compare production for use with production for profit, as it is to compare a red dress with a long dress, or to compare the dress with the party at which it is to be worn. They are not comparable. But, they are reconcilable and each serves its purpose. Together, they give us what we want.

Even more serious is the mistaken concept of the profit motive itself. The root of the error lies in the arbitrary definition given to the profit itself and the consequent notion that it is necessary to do away with profit and the profit motive in order to protect individuals and groups against the exactions of unearned profits or undeserved benefits.

A typical and well-written example of the fallacious teaching, however well-meant, is to be found in a pamphlet issued by the Commission of Social Action of the Evangelical and Reformed Church, issued as long ago as March of 1941, entitled "The Christian and the Profit Motive." The author is Elmer J. F. Arndt. It was written originally as part of the Report of the Commission on Social Action for the Fourth Meeting (1940) of the General Synod of the Evangelical and Reformed Church under the authorization of the Fourth General Synod as "the basis for discussion in our church groups."

The author of this pamphlet defines the profit-motive as "the desire for a reward *beyond* what is truly earned." And, following this strikingly fallacious assumption he says: "To say that men will not work without the hope of profit is to say that men will not work unless they hope to get more than they actually earn." Again, he says: ". . . the profit-motive is contrary to the Christian ethics," and that "The profit-motive cannot be Christianized." He pronounces correctly that "The profit-motive is the dynamic of the profit-system," but gives only half of the fact, for it is a profit *and* loss system; and he does not reach far enough, for the profit-motive is also the dynamic of the production and exchange system. I have already shown that there can be no exchange unless both parties believe they profit by an exchange.

And he is mistaken when he states that "profit is not a reward for service." There are other mistaken statements and inferences in the pamphlet, due to ignorance of economic facts. The pamphlet deserves study, however, because it is apparently sincere and undoubtedly accepted as "gospel truth" by some people, because of its source, and especially by those who *want* to believe denunciations of our economic order. To the author's closing exhortation, "Give us this day our daily bread—so our Lord taught us to pray. Woe to us if, praying this prayer, we snatch bread from the mouth of our fellow-man." I would say amen and add my exhortation to those who set up straw men to denounce that which they do not understand, thus: "Thou shalt not bear false witness . . . woe to us if, while praying to God, we deceive His children and make it difficult to procure the bread for which they pray."

The first error of the author is to define the profit-motive incorrectly, and that error grows out of his mistaken conception of what profit is. Profit is not something above and beyond what a person deserves. It is something above and beyond the cost of production, which is a very different thing. Oddly enough, in his own statements, on page 8 of the pamphlet, Mr. Arndt includes *interest on investment* as part of the cost in an illustrated operation of a business. But the United States Government does not agree with Mr. Arndt and refuses to let this item of interest on investment be considered as part of the cost. *It is part of the profit* which is taxed by government.

But, whether or not "interest on investment" is rightly considered as part of the cost, or should be looked on as part of undifferentiated profit, in either case Mr. Arndt has in effect admitted that there must be payment made for the use of tools owned and furnished by the owners of a business. And that is what profit is, in large part, except that it comes only out of what is left after all costs of running the business have first been paid. And it is the risk of there being nothing left that makes it necessary to consider profit in a different category than interest, which is paid to lenders whether or not the business has anything left afterward for its owners. Profit is payment for that risk.

The profit motive is a desire for benefit, and that desire can be gratified by giving each party to an exchange a benefit above what he yields in the exchange. The fact that BOTH parties to an exchange benefit or profit by the exchange demonstrates that there can be profit without extending beyond what is earned or deserved, as Mr. Arndt has mistakenly claimed.

There is a companion error in the pamphlet in the failure to see that no human impulse need be entirely good or entirely bad. Properly used, the human attributes can be blessings. Improperly used, or carried to extremes, the same attributes can become a curse. Thus, the spirit of acquisitiveness, the stem of an instinct, as I shall show a little later, is necessary to life itself. But, carried to extremes, it becomes the spirit of greed. Desire to benefit is necessary to life itself but it can be carried to the point of covetousness. *And covetousness does not owe its origin or function to the profit and loss system,* or to what Mr. Arndt calls mistakenly "the profit system." It can and will enter into ANY system with the human beings who operate within that system.

To illustrate: the profit-motive is like unto the motor of an automobile. It will take you to church. The same motor will take you to a gambling den. The motor does not choose *where* the car is to go. It only furnishes power. It is the steering wheel that directs the course of the car. So, the profit-motive furnishes the power in economic life. Just as the motor in the automobile is guided in its direction by the steering wheel, so the profit-motive drives in the direction de-

termined by the personal ethics or religion of the human being who
is being propelled. What Mr. Arndt should examine is not the profit-
motive which powers our economic system, but the philosophy of life
or the religion of the people he believes guilty of taking bread out
of the mouths of others, or of so misleading people as to lower the
prospects of having bread at all.

If the profit-motive is contrary to Christian ethics and cannot be
Christianized, then Jesus was guilty of violating His own teachings.
The parable of the talents then loses its manifest and fullest significance. Jesus himself proclaimed that a man was foolish to give up
his soul in exchange for the world, because there was no benefit or
profit for the man in such an exchange. He even recommended cast-
ing into outer darkness the "unprofitable servant," who failed to
return to his master something over and above what the master had
entrusted to him.

I offer no apology for the profit-motive. With full awareness of its
possible implications, I recognize the profit-motive as the most essential
and effective urge in the economic life of man, reaching even to other
phases of his life as he seeks to subdue the earth and gain dominion
over all other creatures.

I do not *propose* the profit-motive. I *accept* the profit-motive as
given by God and implanted in the very vitals of the creature man.
In the very nature of things the profit-motive is basic to life itself.
Implanted at the very core of man, it is the basic urge to life, the
instinct of self-preservation, expressed economically as the spirit of
acquisition, the desire for benefit, or the profit-motive. It is this same
profit-motive that is refined and made even more effective when Jesus
orients it with the law of mutuality of interest as expressed in the
Golden Rule.

We know that struggle is the essence of existence. So long as
there is movement there is life. When movement stops life has fled.
But movement can continue only so long as energy is being released.
And for life to continue, energy must be renewed in at least as great
quantity as it is expended, for life IS the continuing expenditure of
energy by that which lives. If there is to be protection against unanticipated hazards, or if there is to be growth the intake of energy
must be greater than the outgo. And it is from this surplus or profit
that growth and development come. It is only so that a creature desig-

nated by God to subdue the earth and gain mastery over other creatures can fulfill his destiny.

Even the seed that swells with moisture which it absorbs from the ground, and then bursts and sends a tiny shoot above ground while it builds a root below, has more than mere movement for its manifestation of life. It takes on! It adds to itself or accrues. It grows through the process of accretion. It takes in more than it expends; there is a profit!

The infant man is born unseeing and helpless, puny and small. There is movement. With the very first breath of life the child begins to struggle and starts the growth that ultimately brings it to manhood or womanhood. Sometimes the struggle has to be induced or initiated by the physician attending the birth, by holding the infant by its feet and slapping it smartly across the buttocks to make sure that it takes its first gasp and gulp of air and so begins to breathe. The long struggle has begun.

From that time on the process is one of accretion, adding steadily to the materials and potential energy which the child needs for growth. This means that there must be more energy taken in than is expended in the processes we call life. If the child receives only enough food, potential energy, to replace the energy actually expended in the movements of living, it will remain the same size, add nothing to its stature, strength or understanding. Under such conditions it would never mature and become the means of carrying the race through another generation. Mankind would perish from the face of the earth.

In order that there be growth there must be a residue left from the total energy taken in. This residue is a surplus, or, in effect, a profit, which is then invested in growth. It is a surplus of income over outgo, a return of income over cost of production, and without it there can be no growth.

What is true of the body is no less true of the mind, and there is no good reason why it should not also be true of the soul. We grow by accretion.

Nor is there any sensible conflict between this concept and the accepted truth of physics that the amount of energy and matter in the universe remains the same, that matter and energy can change in form, time and place, but not in amount total in the universe.

With the profit that results from economic surplus and accretion we do not deal merely with matter, moving in time and place and changing in form, as well as in possession. We deal also with the exchange of goods and services, with degrees of usefulness to different individuals who have widely varying ideas of what is useful and to what degree. By changing the form of material, or combining one with another to produce a new combination of material, we neither increase nor decrease the quantity of matter or of energy in the world. But we do increase the usefulness or ability of the several materials within the new form or combination to satisfy human wants. We do create utility or the ability to satisfy wants, which is an attribute of things already existing.

The utility of the resulting product may be, and usually is, greater than the mere sum of the separate usefulness of the several elements of which it is composed. The amount by which the resulting utility is greater than would have been the total utility of the separate parts, less the cost of producing it, *is profit*. And the amount of that profit is normally a measure of the efficiency of the individual or organization producing it.

The profit utility so created is more than the product of human labor applied to natural resources. It is created in great part by the effectiveness of tools and machines, which have increased the results of human productivity about one hundred times from the days of the bare-hand savage to the tool-equipped and power-using modern man. Thus profit comes as a result of and is logically a reward for the use of tools in production.

How much of the reward *should* go to the owners of tools, and how much actually *does* go, will be discussed in a later chapter, but here we must understand that profit is a reward for the use of tools and machinery in production, enhanced or diminished by the kind of management which guides the process.

Without affecting one iota of the total quantity of matter and energy in the universe, we have increased enormously the usefulness of natural resources through changing their form or by transferring them from one place or one time to another. It is so that man subdues the earth, a process that is only begun. The undeveloped possibilities stagger the imagination.

The materials from mountains and gravel pits, economically useless to man in their primal form and location, have become enormously useful in the form of roads. Rock and sand, dreary in their primitive monotony, provide the materials for walks, tall buildings, bridges and other structures that constitute our cities. The forests have become furniture, houses and other structures whose building took millions of forest monarchs billions of miles to fashion them into lumber. From the depths of the sea and earth we have brought fourth a bewildering array of materials for manufacture. Ore has been burned free of dross to leave malleable metal, made in turn into coins, ornaments, structural parts, rails for transportation, containers and a myriad of other uses. From those metals have come millions of miles of wire to carry current made by burning coal, oil and gas, to light lamps made from molten sand and other materials. By the work of man, using tools, wisely managed and directed, we have added enormously to the usefulness of crude materials and forces, and we express that utility in terms of the articles which we fashioned.

The wood that goes into an office desk, worth perhaps two dollars in the tree before the tree is cut, represents more than a hundred dollars of value-measured utility in the finished desk ready to install in an office. And that is true even though the quantity of matter remains unchanged. It is utility that we create, the surplusses of which over cost of production constitute profits and are due in large measure to the tools and management that make human energy more effective in producing from natural resources.

This surplus, or profit, excess of utility income realized from intake over outgo, can in truth be called the "genesis of civilization." The spirit of acquisition, born of the instinct of self-preservation, resulting in desire for some article or service in exchange for something one already has or expects to get, or for services available for rendering, in short the profit-motive, is utterly essential to the continuation of the very processes of life and certainly to the exchanges that yield us the increase in utilities from which we improve our well-being.

And yet the author of the booklet referred to on previous pages makes the astounding claim that the consequences of the process of profits are appalling, that it has given us "poverty in the midst of plenty," with the accompanying horror that "over fifty percent of the children in the United States have inadequate clothing, shelter and medical care." Understanding and vision have failed to reveal to him how much better we live in consequence of the very system he denounces! And unhappy those who would have us discard that system for others in use elsewhere in the world, where the rich may well envy our poor!

For, with all the shortcomings of men who have failed to make the best and most just use of their freedom in the United States, we have nevertheless provided for ourselves about seven times our share of the world's goods on the basis of our population. With less than seven percent of the people in the world, we have about 45% of all the wealth and income in the world. And we have substantially increased the share of that income going to workers.

Destroy profit today, and tomorrow the school, the church and all else that is more than subsistence level of living must disappear, and mankind will drop back once more into the morass of savagery. It is thus that the power to tax is the power to destroy, undue taxes preventing investment of the funds otherwise available for continued and increasing productivity of industry, as well discouraging the most effective incentive to endeavor in any field of action.

d. The Actors in Exchange:

The customer is king.

If there is unemployment it is because the customer does not buy the products of the employer in sufficient quantities to keep the employer busy. If there is a shortage of labor in any particular concern it is likely due to the fact that customers of that concern or of other concerns in the same labor market buy so much of the product that the employer has to have more employes to produce enough goods for his market.

The fate of a business rests finally in the hands of its customers. If the customers remain loyal and other customers join their ranks and they all buy more of the products, the manufacturer and those who work for him will prosper and have employment. If the customers reduce or even stop their buying, and buy the products of other concerns instead, the manufacturer will lose money and the workers will lose their jobs. That is why selling is so important to the life of a business, and why a very substantial part of the activity of a business is in the sales and advertising departments. Competition unceasingly demands more and more efficiency in both making and selling.

In consequence the consumer, who is the customer, in America gets more for an hour of work than does the consumer in any other country in the world. In order to prosper, the producer must do an increasingly good job in wooing the consumer. Competition makes the customer king in America because freedom of choice enables the consumer to become a customer for what and whom he will.

But there is another and exceedingly significant aspect to that situation. *The producer and consumer are the same person.* In an economy based on exchange, among free men and women in a free country, we live almost literally by taking in each other's washing. It has already been explained that, as we progress from the utterly primitive individually self-sufficient economy to the greater production that follows specialization of work and use of tools under direction of management, each of us can secure the goods and services he wants only by exchanging his good or service for the good or service produced by someone else. I am your customer and you are my customer. I am the producer of what I make and sell to you, and I am the consumer of what you make and sell to me. Most of us are producers and all of us are consumers: and that makes us all customers.

With the exception of those who live on the fruits of savings which they inherited or themselves accumulated out of their past earnings or income, and most of those employed in government, practically all of our people belong in the category of workers who are both producers and consumers. After we have made due allowance for that part of the total cost of goods which is payment for the accumulation and use of tools and the protection of property and rights by government, we have probably 85% of the total volume of consumption goods business transacted among and by workers. They constitute the great buying public. They produce the goods for the buying public which they themselves constitute. They are their own and each other's customers.

This is tremendously important because it leads us to the workers themselves when we seek answers to questions involving the standard of living, holding prices within reach of wages or dealing with problems of unemployment. To a large extent these problems, along with many others, cannot be solved without taking into consideration measures and attitudes which the workers take toward each other in their reciprocal and dual capacities of producers and consumers, employer and employe, seller and buyer. The customer-consumer is the real boss who provides or refuses work to the employes by buying or refusing to buy the products of other workers. Management is the middleman who manages the process in which the real actors are workers as producers and consumers.

In buying the products made by other workers, the workers as customers limit the number of dollars which can be paid to the workers as producers. Put the shoe on the other foot, and the workers themselves, as producers and sellers, limit the quantity of goods which can be had for their dollars by other workers as consumers.

It follows that, by refusing to buy the products of industry, the workers as customers (consumers) cut off the source of income from which other workers, as producers or sellers, must receive their income: and, by refusing to produce or by raising the cost of production, the workers as producers cut down the quantity of goods which other workers as consumers will be able to buy with their wages, or receive in exchange for their work.

Many people do not appreciate this important fact because one group of workers produce their goods for groups of workers other than themselves, people whom they do not know and probably never see, and the worker producers and the worker consumers are not the identical people as far as any one product is concerned. But they *are* all workers, all of them are producers and all consumers, and all together they buy what all of them produce, making allowance for the 15% or so that is paid for the use of tools and taken by government for taxes.*

When one group of workers, as producers, have their wage rates increased, or receive more money than before for doing no more work and without raising production in the same proportion as the increase in wage rates, some *other* groups of workers, as consumers buying the products of the workers whose wage rates have been so increased, have to pay a larger percentage or portion of their wages for these particular goods; and they have left less money than they would otherwise have had to buy other goods. The consequence is that the customer workers suffer a decrease in their standard of living, since their wages are able to buy less goods than before.

---

*There is apparently a paradox in that the government takes only part of the above 15% of the total national income, whereas the Federal Government alone is said to take more than 30% of the national income in taxes. That is because the government takes taxes out of wages, salaries, interest, rent and profits after these shares have been determined, enough to make the total take by government the approximate 30% of the total income.

Then, if one of the groups of workers who have just suffered as consumers, follows suit and raises the wage rates of its members without raising their production by the same proportion, the first group of workers, who began the increase of wage rates, now suffers at the hands of the second group and takes from them the same kind of punishment which it first dealt out, because the second group is now the producer charging higher prices for the same products bought from them by the first group.

And, when all of the groups follow the same course of action, raising their rates of pay without giving more goods for the more money, *all* of the workers wind up by cutting each others' throats, economically speaking. And they are no better off than they were before the cycle of wage rate increases began. That is exactly what happened in consequence of the so-called cycles of wage increases during the period 1946 through 1948. Three rounds of wage rate increases failed to solve the problem of threatened lower standards of living, and we could have had a hundred such increases and come no nearer to the solution, *so long as production did not increase commensurately with wages.*

It is the function of management, as pointed out in a previous chapter, to secure the most efficient utilization of *all* factors in production, the application of human energy to natural resources, with tools, to the end that workers get more money as producers and get more goods for their money as consumers. That is the process which made America the most prosperous nation in the world.

But the actors in exchange are the workers themselves, constituting the vast majority of our population and probably accounting in their wages and salaries for more than 85% of all the cost of production. So it is literally true that any group or individual which reduces the effectiveness of human energy applied to natural resources in the production of goods and services, eventually harm themselves as well as the rest by so doing, for workers and consumers are the same people, consumers are customers, and the customer is king!

e. The Machinery of Exchange:

Those who specialize and produce goods in quantities more than sufficient for their own needs, cannot enjoy the benefits of the higher standard of living thus made possible unless they can dispose of the surplus of their goods in exchange for the surplus of goods which they do not produce but do need. They must have assurance that they will be able to secure the raw materials out of which they make their goods, which raw materials may have to be secured or produced by someone else. They must have food, clothing and shelter in order to live while they are producing and before they have disposed of their separate products. The answer to every one of these needs is the exchange of goods and services.

BARTER

In its simplest form, and for many generations, exchange was carried on by what is called "barter." In barter one person transfers or hands over his article or personal service to another person who, in turn, transfers or hands over his article or personal service to the first person. It was barter when the hunter, who had caught two rabbits, handed a rabbit over to the fisherman who had caught four fish, and received from the fisherman two fish in exchange for the rabbit. In consequence of the barter, each had two fish and one rabbit.

Later, some other individual acquired a supply of carrots. He had more carrots than he could eat and wanted some fish and some rabbits, either or both. He could barter with one person for fish and with the other for rabbits, provided they would take his carrots in exchange. Still later, additional individuals joined the process of acquiring and bartering still other products or personal services. The products might be wheat, cattle, articles of clothing, tools, the services of a tool maker, and so on. Personal services might include the repairing of nets, cleaning of fish, making of bows and arrows or repairing them, the setting of a broken arm, cutting of hair, and so on. In each case there was the transfer of something by each of two parties to the exchange, each relinquishing ownership of that he gave and acquiring ownership of that which he accepted in exchange for it.

But, useful as was the service rendered by barter, especially in fostering specialized production in its early stages and thereby inaugurating the march of civilization, it suffered from two serious handicaps which limited its usefulness and thereby delayed the growth of civilization itself until the handicaps were overcome.

THE STANDARD OF VALUE

The first handicap in barter was the difficulty of determining the ratio of exchange between the articles or goods, or the amount of one article or personal service that must be given in exchange for one unit of another. There was need of a common language of value, some common denominator in terms of which the ratios of exchange of all commodities and services could be stated. Before men could have any commercial relations they needed a common language of value so they could understand each other. What finally defeated the insurrectionists at the building of the Tower of Babel was that they suddenly all spoke different languages and, failing to understand each other, their efforts became futile.

A common language of value is essential in the carrying on of exchange. Even in the primitive society, the hunter and the fisherman and those who followed with wheat, cattle and other products, would likely understand only his own particular commodity or service. One would think in terms of rabbits, another of fish, still another in terms of wheat, and so on through the list. But, if it happened that all of them desired and knew wheat in addition to his own particular product, then they could all state the values or exchange ratios of their own particular products in terms of wheat.

So, wheat might be worth 100 bushels for one cow, one bushel for one rabbit and half a bushel for one fish. These three values could be spoken of respectively as 100 for the cow, 1 for the rabbit and $\frac{1}{2}$ for the fish. The rabbit hunter would expect to give 100 rabbits for a cow, but also to receive two fish for one rabbit.

The article whose value serves as common denominator, or in terms of which we express other values, in this case a bushel of wheat, is called the standard of value. Strictly speaking, the standard of value is wheat, and the bushel of wheat is the *unit of value*. It is the first basic requirement in any system of exchange beyond barter. It facilitates the making of exchanges just as a common language of words facilitates the exchange of ideas and makes it possible for people to live and cooperate in communities.

Back of the need for a common denominator or language of value is the problem of determining the relative value or desirability of the various goods and services to be exchanged. It is basic in determining the individual share to go to each of the producers of every product which is produced through the cooperation of more than one person.

MEDIUM OF EXCHANGE

The second handicap in barter was that each person wishing to exchange his goods or services, had to find another person who wanted what the first person had to offer and who had to offer what the first person wanted.

Thus: suppose we were using barter today. If I wanted a hair-cut I would go to a barber and ask him to give me a hair-cut. He has plenty of them and can easily furnish me with one, but that is only one half of the transaction. I must give him something for the hair-cut. Alas, I make my living making speeches, so all I can offer him is a five-minute speech in exchange for the hair-cut. But he does not want my speech. He has plenty of his own, gives one free with every hair-cut. So I have to find someone who will accept my speech and give me in exchange for that speech something else which the barber will accept in exchange for the hair-cut.

Perhaps I can find a farmer who will unite with other farmers to listen to one of my speeches and the group will give me some potatoes in exchange for the speech. The barber who did not want my speech does have to eat, so he will accept some potatoes in exchange for the hair-cut. The potatoes become the medium through which a speech can be exchanged for a hair-cut.

The handicap suffered by barter was removed when the barber was willing to accept potatoes in exchange for the hair-cut, and I found a group of farmers who were willing to give me potatoes in exchange for giving them a speech. Even though the barber already had all the potatoes he needed for his own use at the time, he might still be willing to take more potatoes in payment or exchange for the hair-cut, because he could take his surplus potatoes to someone else, who also had to eat, and exchange the potatoes for something which that person had to offer which the barber wanted or could use. Thus, the commodity which a number of people needed from time to time, and so were willing to accept in exchange for their own commodities or services, served as a go-between in the making of several exchanges. This is the step which distinguishes what used to be a "barter economy" from what later became a medium of exchange or "money economy."

The medium of exchange became a tool which man used to facilitate or improve the process of making exchanges. Money for its purpose is just as much a tool as is the drill which bores holes in sheets of steel. It is used to create utility or to make human energy more effective.

MEDIUM OF EXCHANGE SOLVES OTHER DIFFICULTIES

There are two additional difficulties in the making of exchange under barter which the medium of exchange solves, and which should be discussed before we can go on to discuss the elements or instrumentalities through which the exchanges are made with a medium of exchange.

The first of these is that the articles to be exchanged are unequal in value. Thus: suppose that a cattle raiser wants a hair-cut, and the barber wants some beef. Neither of the two problems thus far discussed exists in this situation. Each has what the other wants and understands the value of both articles. But the cow is worth several hundred hair-cuts and the cattle raiser cannot use all the hair-cuts which the cow is worth any more than the barber can eat an entire cow. There is needed a medium of exchange for which the cattle raiser can exchange his entire cow, and of which he can use a small portion to exchange for a hair-cut. The barber can then use this "small portion" of the medium of exchange to buy his roast beef from the man who bought the entire cow from the cattle raiser.

There are other alternatives, but none of them permit the simple trade of a hair-cut for a roast of beef without serious embarrassment to either of the two traders.

The second difficulty occurs when one of the two parties to the exchange, while willing to give up part of his surplus on hand, does not want anything else at the moment, and it becomes necessary to find a way of storing what he wants until later when he wants it. If the barber is willing to give a hair-cut, but does not want any beef now, it is easy, for he can wait until the cattle raiser kills a cow and then he will get his roast beef in payment for the hair-cut already delivered. But, if the cattle raiser is willing to deliver the roast beef now, but does not want any hair-cut now, he must find a way of preserving his right to a hair-cut until he wants it.

In many ways, man has experienced the same need for storing or accumulating goods for the future, or being able to preserve his surplusses until he could use them or exchange them.

Unless there were some way of preserving either the accumulated goods, or the purchasing power in other goods for which they had been exchanged, the risks of saving would be so great that there would be no accumulation of goods or savings. Man would never have risen above a hand-to-mouth standard of living, glutting himself in periods of plenty and starving in periods of scarcity.

Man accumulated purchasing power, or wealth, long before he had money as we know it now, and it was much more difficult to preserve and protect. Job was known to be wealthy by the number of kine, asses and camels, and other animals he had accumulated. He prospered exceedingly, but almost in the twinkling of an eye, overnight, the Sabeans stole his oxen, fire burned up his sheep, and the Chaldeans carried away his camels and even the servants who tended them. His wealth was gone!

Jacob was worth a great fortune when he departed from Laban, his father-in-law. So great was his wealth that he could easily afford to give his brother Esau two hundred she-goats, twenty he-goats, two hundred ewes, twenty rams, thirty milch camels with their colts, forty kine, ten bulls, twenty she-asses and ten foals, as a present to ward off his wrath. Esau with his four hundred men might have despoiled Jacob of his entire wealth and left him destitute. Wealth of that kind was not easily preserved.

Today wealth is vastly more secure and certain in the many moderate fortunes which ensure comfortable retirement in old age. But, while the forms of wealth have gone through many changes, gradually becoming more secure and easily protected, wealth still is not permanent. What we have done is to make it more mobile, somewhat more stable in value and make it more difficult for thieves to steal or enemies to destroy. Law and order protecting private property and the right of contract, more durable and fluid forms of wealth, have encouraged saving and investment, and vastly increased production over those of the days of Jacob and Job. But the problem is far from finally solved.

Qualities of "Money"

While the functions of Standard of Value and Medium of Exchange are clear and distinct, it so happens that whatever serves in either capacity must possess qualities essential to the other. For that reason, especially in their early history, a single commodity served as both Standard of Value and Medium of Exchange.

For a common language of value we needed a single commodity as a standard for estimating and comparing values and in terms of which to express the ratios of exchange. Such a commodity must have been widely used and frequently exchanged, so that people could become familiar with it and know its value in terms of other commodities.

That same commodity, being widely used and well-known, frequently exchanged, was also the logical and natural choice to serve as a medium of exchange. It is apparent that such a commodity must be acceptable to everyone, and, consequently, the basic and vitally essential characteristic or quality of that commodity can be called "Universal Acceptability."

In a primitive community "universal acceptability" might be an attribute of a number of commodities, including cattle, horses, wheat and even shells from the sea shore. But, as civilization advanced and the volume and variety of goods produced and exchanged increased and became more complex, the very commodities which at first possessed universal acceptability because everyone used them and exchanged them, were no longer acceptable in the same degree. On the other hand, new instrumentalities, some of them not even consumed as commodities, became universally acceptable and so qualified to serve as a medium of exchange.

With the tremendous increase in number and variety of exchanges, it became increasingly important that exact equivalents be exchanged. Therefore the medium of exchange must be accurate and capable of transferring the exact amount of value involved in the transaction. The same development called increasingly for convenience in the making of transfers. And the growing importance of saving, or storing purchasing power to later times, and the greater frequency and extent of time lapse between selling and buying, or buying and selling, made it important that the medium of exchange be safe: that is, retain all of the value exchanged for it until that value could be exchanged for something else at a later time.

To meet the combined needs of universal acceptability, accuracy, convenience and safety, the commodity which serves as combined standard of value and medium of exchange must meet the following requirements:

> 1. It must possess usefulness and *value as a commodity,* quite apart from its use as a standard of value or medium of exchange. As a one-foot rule must possess length in order

to be used as a measure of length, so the monetary standard must possess value in order to be used to measure values of other commodities.

2. It must have *stability of value.* Otherwise, someone who accepts it in exchange for some personal service or other commodity, intending to keep it until he needs or wants something else, may discover later that the value, or purchasing power, has gone down and he is not able to buy as much as he could have bought if he had spent the purchasing power as soon as he received it. On the other hand, he may have borrowed some medium of exchange (money) from someone else who has a surplus, or accumulation from his savings. Later, the borrower will have to pay back what he borrowed. If, in the meantime that value in the money has gone up, the borrower will have to do more work, or sell more commodities in order to secure the money with which to pay back what he borrowed. If the value of money had gone down after the loan was made, the borrower would gain and the lender would lose when the debt was paid.

In justice to all parties to exchange, at all times, it is highly desirable that the value of money remain the same over long periods of time.

3. It must be *durable.* Anything passed from hand to hand many times in payment of purchases or the making of exchanges, will wear and lose some of its value unless it is durable. It should not be easily perishable, or it cannot retain its value until the person who saves it uses it later for other transactions.

4. It should be *divisible* into many grades of value, so that every possible transaction, of any amount, can be carried on with it. There should be different denominations, or fixed amounts of value, so that by combining them any possible amount of value from minute to enormous can easily be transferred.

5. It must be capable of containing *high value in small bulk* and be easily and safely carried or transported. This is not as easy as might seem. For example, a diamond would meet this requirement because an enormous total of value

could be carried in a very small package, but the diamond would not meet other requirements as well. The very fact that it contains very high value in small bulk would prevent it from serving as a medium of exchange in small value transactions, because it could not be cut up into smaller portions without destroying a large part of the value it now has before it is divided. Thus, cut into ten parts, each exact tenth of that diamond would have less value than one tenth of the value of the whole diamond.

6. Finally, it must be *easy and convenient to recognize* and distinguish from other commodities or monetary instruments. It must be possible to know at a glance how much value the piece of money represents, so as to minimize cheating and facilitate rapid exchange. This attribute we call *cognizability.*

The qualities of *possessing commodity value, stability of value* and *durability* are indispensable to the standard of value. However, we have learned that to make the medium of exchange adequately *durable, divisible, transportable in large amounts* and *cognizable,* it is necessary to use instruments, such as cheaper coins, paper money and credit instruments, which cannot serve as the standard of value. To overcome this difficulty and enable the monetary instruments to keep their full exchange value they should be redeemable at their face value in the standard of value.

Of all the commodities used as standard of value through the years, gold and silver have proved the best because of their durability, high value, divisibility, easy cognizability and relative stability of value. While less desirable than gold, where it is available in greater quantities silver has served as standard of value as well as medium of exchange. China and India are examples of countries which have so used silver. In other countries, which had enough gold to serve both as standard of value and medium of exchange, people preferred to use gold and found it the better form of money.

The discovery of gold in Mexico and South America by the Spanish explorers and later exploiters, was followed by a period of tremendous prosperity for Spain. Europe needed gold desperately to facilitate the larger number of exchanges resulting from her growing volume of industry and commerce. The gold was needed also as a means of storing wealth in a form easily moved and readily accepted. The gold that Spain spent in maintaining her huge armies and carrying on war in Europe, stayed behind when the armies were finally drawn back to Spain, and furnished the basis of future monetary systems in Europe.

Having adopted gold as the standard of value, the next step was to determine or define the amount of gold which should constitute the unit of value. It would be impossible to state values in terms of any commodity until a unit, or specific quantity of that commodity, had been designated as the unit by which to measure the value.

In the United States we defined a "dollar" as the unit of value, to consist of 23.22 grains of pure gold. This was combined with 2.58 grains of copper to make the standard dollar of 25.80 grains in weight and was so used for many years. The copper increased the durability of the coin. In 1934, using power given him by the Congress for the purpose of raising domestic prices and encouraging foreign purchases of our goods, President Franklin D. Roosevelt changed this standard dollar to 15.23 grains in weight, containing 13.71 grains of pure gold and 1.52 grains of copper. One ounce of gold now weighs, or contains 35 times as much as the amount of pure gold in the new dollar. Therefore the new dollar is said to be one thirty-fifth of an ounce and gold is quoted at $35.00 an ounce. An ounce of pure gold weighs 480 grains. When the 480 grains of pure gold in an ounce was divided by 23.22 grains of the former dollar, we had 20.67 dollars in each ounce of gold, and gold was worth $20.67 an ounce before Mr. Roosevelt depreciated the dollar.

We avoid confusion if we remember that Mr. Roosevelt did not depreciate gold itself. He lowered the amount of gold in the unit of value, our dollar, and thus depreciated the dollars. That raised prices by making it necessary to pay more dollars for a given amount of value in goods.

When we say that an article is worth ten dollars we are saying that the value of the article is ten times as much as the value contained in the number of grains of gold that constitute a dollar, or the unit of value.* And, just as it now takes $35.00 instead of $20.67 to buy

---

*This relationship exists early in the development of a monetary system and will continue so long as there is a free frequent exchange of gold for other forms of goods. The tendency is for the relationship to become obscured as other forms of money (medium of exchange) develop, even though those other forms or instruments are kept redeemable in the standard of value. The standard of value (gold) is used less and less as

an ounce of gold, because of the smaller amount of gold in the new dollar, it also takes more of the new dollars to buy the same goods that could be bought by fewer of the old value dollars with more gold in them, and prices go up.

As was bound to happen anywhere that men relied upon exchange to disseminate the products of industry, with profit to be made in buying and selling goods, moving them from places where they were less valuable to other places where they were more valuable, or changing their form to increase their utility, or holding them until their value had increased, men learned also to trade in the money itself.

Persons who were capable of cheating in trading goods, found it just as easy and often more profitable to cheat in exchanging moneys. Coins could be clipped, or remelted and mixed with other metals of less value. This practice offered its greatest possibilities when anyone was permitted to mint metal into coins, resulting in a bewildering confusion of different kinds of coins.

It was found necessary to have standard coins, certified and guaranteed by some authority acceptable to people who used the coins. Therefore, it was only natural that governments, wherever they existed, early took over the prerogative and function of providing the money of a country.

In the United States, for example, the Constitution provides that Congress shall have the exclusive power to "coin money and regulate the value thereof." The founders of our country recognized that the coining of money is properly a government monopoly to provide the country with a uniform and honest system of money.

It was clearly the intent of the founders of our government that our federal government should make only money of metal, or coins. And by regulating the value thereof they meant determining the value of the unit, or the amount of metal to be minted in the coin. Seventy-five years later, after costly experience with unregulated

---

an actual medium of exchange. Finally, the goods exchanged are really valued in terms of each other, with the ratios of exchange stated in terms of the gold standard unit of value (the dollar). But the actual amount of gold indicated by the number of dollars of price does not necessarily now represent the actual value of the goods. This is particularly true, and leads to dangerous complexity and uncertainty in our monetary system, when the standard commodity, gold, is actually withdrawn from circulation and forbidden to the possession by our citizens, as was done by passage of the gold prohibition law in 1934.

state banks issuing paper money and with the problem of financing the war between the States, our Federal Government began the issuance of paper money, first government notes and then other forms, making them legal tender and requiring people to accept them in payment of debt, public and private.

By fixing a certain amount of gold as the unit of value (dollar), and providing free coinage of gold, thereby permitting anyone to bring gold bullion to the mint to be made into money in the form of gold coins, the United States established gold as the standard money. The government, while making no charge for the minting of the coins, did charge for the alloy of copper that was mixed with the gold to make it wear better.

For the sake of convenience and to provide smaller denominations which could not practically be made of gold, the government also made coins out of cheaper metals. Contrary to its practice with gold coin, the government made the cheaper metal coins with a higher face value than their actual metal content could justify. To keep the coins in circulation at their face value, these lesser denominations were made redeemable in gold at their face value and limited in the amounts in which they could serve as legal tender. The one exception was the silver dollar, which contained less than its face value in metal, but which was given unlimited legal tender.

Paper bills can be printed in any denomination merely by using different figures for the amounts designating their face value, and are a very convenient way of carrying much money in small bulk. A one thousand dollar bill takes no more room and weighs no more than a one dollar note. But, like coins whose face value is greater than the value of their metal content, paper money would circulate freely and at face value only if people knew that others would accept it. So the paper money had to be redeemable or convertible at face value in gold if it were to be accepted at face value.*

*This is not disproved by the fact that paper money circulates in the United States today in spite of its not being redeemable in gold. We have no money redeemable in gold and must use what there is available. So long as we know there IS gold to redeem the paper money, and so long as Congress refrains from going wild in issuing paper money without more than a government promise to pay behind it, it is likely that we can continue to use our present forms of money, subject to such inflationary forces and effects as are already at work. One of the most effective measures to discourage further inflation would be to repeal the gold prohibition law and permit people of the United States to own gold coin, as well as to present other forms of money to be redeemed in gold coin by the government.

FIDUCIARY MONEY

All money which circulates on faith, in part or in whole, can be called *fiduciary money*. The story of fiduciary money is one of the most fascinating in the history of economics and there is still considerable difference in the views of economists regarding this form of money and its relation to standard money (gold). For our purpose it will suffice to point out here that all money in circulation in our country today is fiduciary money, since the Gold Prohibition Law of 1933 removed gold from circulation and made it a criminal offense for a private citizen to possess gold money.

Today gold is still nominally the standard of value and the basis of our monetary system, and many economists, including the writer, believe it will be necessary to return actually to the free circulation of gold and its uses in settling international trade balances, before our monetary troubles can be over. But actually, gold is no longer a medium of exchange in our domestic economy. It can be imported and exported, but only by permission of the federal government.

Our fiduciary money falls into two classes: coins and paper money.

The coined money includes silver dollars and silver subsidiary coins, half-dollars, quarter-dollars and dimes. Also there are five cent pieces (one twentieth of a dollar) made of alloyed nickle, and pennies (one hundredth of a dollar) made of copper or bronze. The unit is one dollar and the smallest denomination is one hundredth of that dollar, or one cent. The other denominations are five, ten, twenty-five and fifty.

The paper money includes United States notes (greenbacks) which are pure promises to pay the bearer the amount indicated on their face, with no specific security and backed only by the general credit of the government. There are still a few Treasury Notes of 1890 in circulation, some silver certificates in small denominations (mostly one dollar and some fives) redeemable in silver, but the great bulk of our paper currency consists of Federal Reserve Notes issued by the Federal Reserve Banks under supervision of the federal government. Before the gold prohibition law there were also gold certificates, redeemable in gold coin, but these, like gold itself, were taken out of circulation as rapidly as they appeared in banks or fell into government hands.

It is due to faith in our government, but, even more, it is due to custom and habit that our money is accepted at face value. So long as people believe the money is good, and that down in Kentucky there is a huge hoard of gold that could be used to redeem the paper money if necessary, it will probably continue to pass at its face value. There is no better money with which to compare it in purchasing power, and so there is no way of knowing the real measure of our acceptance of it.   .

Then too, the Federal Reserve notes are actually secured by commercial loans and government bonds to the full amount of their face value. They are more than mere promises to pay, or money that circulates because of government fiat. They are in effect mortgages on securities.

What may happen in the future remains to be seen, but if ever people lose faith in our government, and there is no gold at hand to redeem the paper and other elements in our currency, we may see their exchange values drop and prices zoom upward as they do when inflation passes beyond control. There is sound reason in the position of those economists who hold that honesty and good sense require the repeal of the Gold Prohibition Law, and that the people again be permitted to own and use gold for money. This would set up the most effective barrier against possible wild issue of money by a Congress.

LIMITS TO FIDUCIARY MONEY

Money as a medium of exchange and as a means of storing and transporting purchasing power, is limited in efficiency by the ratio of its physical bulk to its total value and by the risks involved in its use.

If the ratio of physical bulk to total value is high, due to low denomination of coin or paper, the amount of purchasing power that can be stored or transported is less. If the ratio is low, the amount of purchasing power that can be stored or transported is greater. But, in any case, no matter how valuable the commodity, or even the paper instruments with fixed denominations, whichever be used as a medium of exchange, a point is reached when the addition of value to be carried takes the total bulk of the medium of exchange so high that the money cannot be conveniently or practically transported, or the risks involved in handling are so great as to forbid its use. It can happen that the cost of handling or transporting the money may reach so deeply into its total value as to forbid its use at all.

There is need for some form of medium of exchange which can carry unlimited total amounts of purchasing power without adding to the bulk of the instruments, and around the use of which there can be thrown adequate safeguards against theft or loss.

CREDIT AS A MEDIUM OF EXCHANGE

Banking and the use of bank credit as a medium of exchange had their origin in a perfectly natural development in the expansion of trade and commerce in the middle ages. As commerce expanded, trading caravans carried small armies with them to protect their gold and goods for exchange. For whatever was useful to the world as a standard of value and medium of exchange, possessing universal acceptability, as well as the goods carried for sale and exchange, was also a prize for the thief and bandit.

There was needed some way of transferring the purchasing power in the gold and other coins of different countries without actually moving the gold or other coins themselves. There was also need for someone expert enough to evaluate accurately the various kinds and denominations and issues of coins of one country along with those of others. These and other reasons were responsible for the growing practice of owners depositing their coins for safekeeping with these experts, the medieval bankers who kept the coins in strong boxes and made a charge for their safe-keeping.

The bankers gave receipts for the coins to those who deposited them, and in course of time the depositors discovered that they could transfer the receipts instead of the coins themselves. They did not need to withdraw the coins from the bankers. So long as the seller of goods had confidence that the receipt was good for the amount of coins named on it, he would accept the receipt in payment for the goods.

Seeing how convenient it was to pass along the receipts instead of the money itself, it was not long before the bankers were issuing the receipts and, confident that these instruments would not be presented immediately, if at all, for redemption, the bankers also loaned out the coins which had been left with them for safe-keeping. This brought in two sources of revenue; one a payment for the safe-keeping of the funds (coins) and the second an interest charge on the coins for their use by borrowers.

Since capital, stored up purchasing power to be used for producing additional goods, especially in the form of tools, is itself productive, the borrowers of the coins could afford to pay the interest charges for the loans. And, as the volume of this branch of the banking business grew, the bankers could afford to accept deposits of coins for safe-keeping without making any charge for that service. The time was to come, many years later, when the loaning of funds became of sufficient volume that the banks could afford to pay interest, or a fee, to the owners of money to induce them to deposit that money with the bank for safe-keeping.

In the above illustration the real instrument of exchange was the "right to demand" funds as certified in the receipt or credit instrument. The credit itself, passing as a medium of exchange with the instrument, consists of the "right to demand."

The range and area as well as the volume of exchange were enormously increased by the use of credit as a medium of exchange. Instead of transporting or transferring some physical form of money which would vary in bulk with the amount of its value, a buyer could give his promise to pay in exchange for goods and services. That promise to pay, which gave the seller and consequent holder of the credit instrument a "right to demand" on the promisor, or purchaser, required no bulk whatever. It is conceivable that the wealth of the world could thus be transferred on a single small piece of paper, or through the record on the books of a bank.

As a medium of exchange, credit is far more convenient than any other form of money. Credit requires no minting of coins, no printing, approval and maintenance of paper instruments. All that is necessary is the recording of a promise to pay which passes as a "right to demand" an equivalent some time in the future. Thus through credit it becomes possible to use character and good will as purchasing power. Men can borrow the savings of other people and use the savings productively to create the very means of repaying the loan some time in the future.

Thus credit has been a tremendous spur to production. Through credit the resources of the future can be put to work in the present, thereby enormously increasing the amount of capital or tools with which to increase the productivity of man working with the materials and forces of nature.

ELASTICITY

In addition to its far greater convenience and safety over any other form of medium of exchange, credit has elasticity, an attribute which is indispensable to the smooth operation of commerce and which attribute is possessed by none of the other forms of medium of exchange in anything like the same degree. It is safe to say that bank credit is the only really elastic element in our monetary system.

By elasticity we mean the ability of the medium of exchange to expand or to contract in volume automatically and immediately wherever necessary, and proportionately to the needs of commerce.

Thus, in the fall of the year in agricultural regions there is usually a pronounced increase in the need for medium of exchange (money) to move the crops. An elastic medium of exchange will immediately expand at the place where the additional funds are needed and place the funds in the hands of those who need them to move the crops, as they need the funds. After the crops are sold, and money comes from various places in payment for them, the medium of exchange which expanded to move them should now contract, since it has served its purpose and is no longer needed in so great amount. The same need for more funds exists when there is industrial need to employ more workers, buy more raw materials and pay other increased costs of doing business. It is important that the medium of exchange expand sufficiently to meet the increased need for funds immediately, exactly where they are needed and come into the hands of those persons who need them, so that there need be no delay in either moving the crops or employing the workers and producing the additional goods.

This need cannot be met by the issue of government money. By the time the authorization is given and action taken by government to get the money made and carried to whom and where it is needed, it is almost certain that the need which occasioned the issue will have passed. And, even though the need still exists when the money is ready, the government cannot forecast just where or in what amounts the medium of exchange needs to expand. Even Federal Reserve notes, which are issued with commercial paper (loans to business for self-liquidating purposes) as security, fail somewhat of the necessary elasticity. The action must be immediate, even automatic and in exact amount for the precise persons who need it. Only bank credit can fill that need.

Without bank credit, or without the modern provisions which make it greatly elastic, funds would be invested in one part of the country and then have to pass suddenly to another part of the country, thereby disrupting one business activity in order to aid another. That was what happened in the earlier days when surplus bank funds were invested in the stock market and had to be moved back to meet demand for crop moving and other needs for additional funds. Money and business panics and even depressions were precipitated by the lack of elasticity when additional funds were needed.

How Credit Comes Into and Goes Out of Existence
as a 'Medium of Exchange
How the Medium Expands

While credit used for purchases on *open book account* serves as a medium of exchange, it is limited to the parties between whom the account exists. Thus, farmer Jones may take his eggs to general store-keeper Smith and get credit on the books of the storekeeper for the eggs delivered to him. The farmer can use that credit ("right to demand") to buy something in Smith's store.

Perhaps the farmer was credited at the rate of fifty cents a dozen for five dozen eggs. His account is credited with $2.50 on Smith's books. Then Jones may buy ten pounds of sugar at ten cents a pound, and five yards of cloth at 22 cents a yard. His account on Smith's books is now charged with $1.00 for the sugar and $1.10 for the cloth, a total of $2.10. So he still has a balance of 40 cents ($2.50 minus $2.10) against which he can buy something else in the store.

But he cannot use that balance of forty cents to buy an ice cream cone at the drug store. That forty cents does not have universal acceptability, since it is acceptable only on the books of Smith the general storekeeper.

On the other hand, when a business man goes to his bank and borrows money to buy raw materials, hire labor or meet some other expense, he simply signs a note, or promise to pay, for the amount he needs, promising to pay it back to the bank within a given time. Three months is a common period of time for such loans. The bank has to make a charge for this service, which is commonly called interest. Strictly speaking, it is a service charge to cover the cost involved in transforming a right to demand funds sometime in the future into rights to demand funds immediately in the present.

If the money is borrowed for three months and the charge is at the rate of six per cent, the banker is likely to deduct $1\frac{1}{2}\%$ (for one-fourth of the year), or $15.00 on a loan of $1,000.00, and place the balance, or $985.00, to the credit of the business man on the books of the bank. This method of loaning is called "Discounting" because it collects the interest in advance. By crediting the business man with $985.00, the bank has actually created that much money, to remain in existence until the note is paid and the amount is then deducted from the account of the business man.

The borrower is now given a book of blank checks, or forms on which he can make out orders to the bank to transfer some or all of his credit on the books of the bank to the person designated on the check as payee. Suppose he buys a ton of coal for' $18.00. He draws a "check" ordering the bank to pay $18.00 to the coal dealer from whom he bought the coal. The coal dealer can then deposit the check with the same bank and have the credit for $18.00 deducted from the business man's account (borrower) and added or credited to the coal dealer's account. Or he can deposit the check in another bank, which bank will then credit the coal dealer with $18.00 and proceed to collect the $18.00 from the bank on which the check was drawn. The first bank then credits the second bank where the check was deposited, with $18.00 and deducts the $18.00 from the account of the borrowing business man who drew the check in the first place. In any case, the credit for $18.00 is transferred from the business man to the coal dealer. The coal dealer may buy a sports jacket for $18.00 and give the check to the haberdasher. Then it is the haberdasher who deposits the check, and the transfer of the funds is made as before. If the sports jacket cost only $16.50, the haberdasher will take the $18.00 check and give the coal dealer $1.50 cash in change.

The $18.00 credit is now on the books of the bank where the haberdasher deposited the check, to the credit of the haberdasher. He may buy something else from another person and give that person a check on his account, and the credit that came into being with the business man borrowing from the bank now serves as medium of exchange for a third or fourth and many more transactions. It is the "right to demand" an equivalent that serves as the medium of exchange. This right to demand differs from the right to demand arising out of a credit entry on the books of our general storekeeper, because a farmer brought in some eggs, in that the open book account credit is good only on the books of that merchant, and for only the farmer to whom it is credited, whereas the bank credit is widely acceptable and can be used anywhere the borrower sees fit to use it.

So much for the expansion of credit. Now comes the converse process.

How the Medium Contracts

The business man, at a later date, having sold the goods whose production he financed by the $985.00 he received by discounting his note for $1,000 at the bank, has built up his deposit credit at the bank by depositing money and other checks which he received in payment for the goods as he sold them. When his note for $1,000 falls due, 90 days after he borrowed the money, he draws a check for $1,000 payable directly to the bank from whom he borrowed it, and gets back the note he signed. Or the bank may simply deduct the $1,000 from his account, with or without a check to the bank.

The important fact, now, is that the bank does not credit the $1,000 to some other person or customer. In consequence, $985.00 of bank credit goes out of existence, and the remaining $15.00 is added to the assets of the bank. The $15.00 which the borrower paid for the services of the bank in loaning him the money, comes out of the income produced by the commercial process, or, if you please, out of the profit created by the commercial process. If business did not create additional wealth through profit arising from the use of capital, the process of creating bank credit would stop. And the total wealth is increased by at least the amount of "interest" (the $15.00) produced and paid by the business man to the bank.

In effect, as a result of this transaction, at least $15.00 of new wealth has come permanently into existence. That is what is meant when the economist states that interest *can* be paid because capital is productive. If this were not true, and the use of money, however secured or created, did not add to the total wealth by at least the amount of interest paid, the amount of tools in use would decline, productivity would decrease and the standard of living would go down. Bank credit has contributed enormously to the increase in the standard of living, even for people who have never stepped inside a bank or used its facilities.

There is room for discussion on the amount of the charge which a bank should make for this service. If too much is charged, it becomes difficult to maintain effective investment or use of our capital, or the bank acquires control over a dangerously high percentage of the capital of a nation. Such a charge could be called "usury." If the amount charged is too small, the bank is unable to meet its expenses and may even go out of business, and the practically indispensable form of medium of exchange called "bank credit" ceases to exist as a medium of exchange.

Normally, competition will take care of the rate charged, with the forces of demand and supply operating there as they do in other fields. Because of the high public interest in the effect of banking on our entire commercial and industrial structure, as well as on individual personal affairs, there is justification for reasonable governmental supervision and regulation of banks.

Interest Really a Service Charge

The fifteen dollars which the bank charged the business man in the example given is usually spoken of as "interest" or the amount of the "discount." Actually it is not interest. It is figured that way, as a percentage of the amount borrowed for whatever period is involved until the borrower pays off his note; but the true nature of the transaction is a "charge" for converting rights to demand in the future into rights to demand immediately on the bank. The business man gives the bank the right to demand $1,000 from him three months from now, and in payment for that right receives from the bank the right to demand $985 from the bank immediately. Because the right to demand on the bank is much more acceptable generally as a medium of exchange than is the right to demand on the business man, and because the right to demand on the business is good some time in the future, whereas the right to demand on the bank is good in the immediate present, the *right to demand on the bank is worth more* and the charge of fifteen dollars really represents the amount by which the bank credit (right to demand on the bank) is worth more than the credit of the business man, as a medium of exchange. The bank is more widely known and the right to demand funds from the bank is immediately available without any loss of time or any question as to its validity.

The so-called interest of fifteen dollars is comparable to the gross margin which is charged by a manufacturer for converting labor and materials into something of greater value by virtue of the new and more useful form he embodies in the resulting product. In much the same way, the bank converts future rights to demand funds from a person into the more useful and valuable present rights to demand funds from the bank.

Making Character into Money

It may be that a banker, having great confidence in the character of a business man, will let him have bank credit for a specific amount in exchange for a note in which the man promises to pay that amount to the bank. In this case the bank may not require additional securities deposited with the bank, which the bank can sell in the event that the man fails to pay his note; and thus character, or confidence in character, has been transmuted into medium of exchange.

But it is not good commercial banking, no matter how good the character of the man, unless the deposit credit given to the man is used to initiate or carry on some industrial or commercial process whose completion will result in the creation of the added wealth which makes it possible to repay the amount of the credit allowed as well as the service charge of the banker (interest collected for loan).

Ideally, the total amount of money or medium of exchange (including the credit instruments) should rise and fall in volume with the total volume of wealth, or combined goods and services, produced and exchanged. If industry and commerce are expanding, the total volume of medium of exchange should do the same, and conversely contract if the volume of exchanges declines. To some extent this adjustment can be made by increasing or decreasing rate of turnover (called "velocity") with a given amount of medium of exchange in use, but there must also be an adjustment in the volume of the medium, or amount of money, to help maintain the stable purchasing power of the dollar.

Because civilization has brought an ever increasing volume of production and consumption, with a continuing increase in the permanent amount of capital or tools used for further production, the total volume of the medium of exchange in use has risen and remained at permanently higher levels.

Banks should be permitted to make other than commercial loans, of course. But these other loans should be made with funds already existing and in possession of the bank. Long time transactions or permanent investments, or any other which do not fall under the classification of self-liquidating commercial transactions should not be used as the means to bring additional medium of exchange into existence as part of the total volume of credit. Commercial loans should be self-liquidating.

At the same time, government should not be permitted, or should not assume the prerogative, to use money issues for any purpose other than to provide and maintain for the country a sound and honest medium of exchange. Too often, governments have debased the coin of a country, taking in good coin and reissuing those coins with an admixture of baser and cheaper metals, for the sake of profit to the government or to the monarch as a means of revenue. Likewise, government should avoid inflating money by printing its own promises to pay, making them legal tender, as a means of paying its bills or raising funds which the public is neither willing nor able to pay in taxes or other forms of government revenue.

The medium of exchange and the standard of value (money in its two basic functions) should be used only for monetary purposes, except that the commodity which serves as a standard of value must be subject to demands upon it as a commodity. Any other use by government is bound to lead to confusion, bad fiscal policies and even corruption. The medium of exchange should serve only for monetary and not be used for fiscal purposes.

THE ROOT OF ALL EVIL

Money itself is not an evil. What has been characterized as the "root of evil" through the ages was not money itself, but the *love of money*. And love of money means love of the things that can be bought with money. Since money became the storehouse of value and purchasing power as well as the medium through which goods and services could be exchanged, it became the means through which men could store power as well as wealth. The very qualities that made it possible for money to serve mankind in the exchange of goods, also gave increased power into the hands of men who sought evil instead of good. The evil or the good was not and is not in the instrument, the money, but in the hands that used the instrument. It would be as reasonable to denounce freedom itself as the root of evil because under freedom the capacities of men are released and expand, increasing power and opportunity for evil as well as for good.

Even Jesus made no effort to do away with monetary systems of the day. He saw evil in the undue love for material things which money itself could be used to buy, but He did not condemn the instrument of exchange itself any more than He condemned the air which was breathed by evil men, or the food they ate and which gave them strength to do evil deeds. He even used the monetary instrument when occasion required.

Money is an indispensable instrument in the development of exchange and all that exchange makes possible. The great problem in the progress of man is to develop his self-discipline and self-command, commensurate with the power and capacity of the instruments at his disposal.

f. Value and Price:

Before goods and services can be exchanged we must determine the ratios at which they are to exchange for each other. These ratios will depend upon how much each article is worth in terms of the others, or how much they are worth in terms of each other. That is the problem of *value.*

But, if the value of each commodity or service is *expressed* in terms of each of the others, we shall have as many different languages of value as there are commodities, and thereby make understanding so difficult as to limit both the area and extent of exchange. We must use a common denominator in terms of which the ratios of exchange of ALL goods and services can be expressed, thus giving us a common language of value. That is the problem of price, for price is the value of a commodity or service expressed in terms of the common standard of value.

THE PROBLEM OF VALUE

Practically all of economics is related to the problem of determining the relative worth of goods and services. It leads us into price and then into wages, interest, rent and profits. Finally, it becomes a problem of control of the economic process. Therefore the core of any theory of economics is its theory of value.

Value is a dangerous word to use. It has many meanings and some of them are so far apart that we have to seek other terms to describe them. Still others are so laden with emotion that we cannot deal with them dispassionately.

Fortunately, no theory of economic value need include the various concepts except as they contribute to or share in the answer to the question: "What is the amount of a commodity or service that must be given in exchange for any other commodity or service?" The real task of the theory of value is to explain *exchange value,* which is the name we give to the amount of anything that must be given in exchange for something else. Thus, if a rabbit exchanges for two fish, the exchange value of each fish is one-half rabbit and the exchange value of the rabbit is two fish.

In a commonly accepted sense, value is an attribute possessed by anything that is of use in satisfying human wants. In this sense there are values in all phases of life, political, social, scientific, ethical, esthetic, cultural, religious, spiritual, material and economic. To the economist, however, this is not yet value. He calls it "utility" or the ability to satisfy human wants. The utility is due to some inherent quality possessed by the thing which has utility. But the article which possesses utility can have economic value, or value in exchange, or exchange value, only if there is also, somewhere, a human want unsatisfied which that utility could satisfy. Under such conditions the article is "scarce" in addition to having utility, and therefore has economic value. If there are no unsatisfied wants for the article it may still have utility, but no scarcity and therefore no economic value.

Thus: air normally is so plentiful that I can get all I want of it without making any effort or giving up anything else in order to get it. No matter where I go there is more air that I need, ready to be breathed. I use all I want of it, and there is still much more left than I can possibly use, even after everyone else takes all he wants of it. Any one unit of air has high utility because it can satisfy an indispensable want. We cannot live without air. But, there is no scarcity, and therefore it has no value in exchange, or in the economic sense. I have no unsatisfied wants for air and so I need not give up anything else to induce someone to give me a unit of air. Therefore it can have no importance in exchange. It is the fact of scarcity added to utility that makes anything important economically. Only then will we esteem it sufficiently to put forth any effort or make any sacrifice to get it.

It has been popular to declaim in favor of an "economy of abundance" rather than an "economy of scarcity." It is a catch phrase that has misled many good people into superficial and erroneous interpretations of economic facts. We *do* want an economy of abundance in that we want more and better things for more and more people. That is what constitutes a higher national standard of living. But to think of abundance in the sense of everyone having everything he wants without paying the necessary price for it, is to conjure up a condition which would erase all values and finally destroy man himself. To have abundance in that sense would remove all incentive. People would stop working and then the abundance itself would disappear, bringing back poverty to a people less able to overcome that poverty in consequence of the easy prosperity previously enjoyed.

Perhaps that is why God did not provide man with many free goods, things existing in quantities sufficient and in form available to satisfy all wants without any effort or work. Except for air and water in most parts of the world, God has made it necessary for man to exert himself to get the things he needs and wants, and even water is not always plentiful. All other goods are scarce and man must work for them.

Scarcity is not a bad word. It is a good word. Work is not a bad word either. It is a good word. Together, these two words point to a basic law of life: it is by overcoming scarcity with work that man enters into his material inheritance, and qualifies for the moral and spiritual development to follow. Far back in the beginnings it was apparently ordained that man should earn his bread in the sweat of his face. All nature teaches us that struggle is the essence of existence. When man stops being active he begins to rot and disintegrate, mentally, spiritually and physically. That is the law of life. To deny it is to deny God.

Indeed, man is so constituted that even if all scarcity were removed at a given moment, it would at once reappear; for the wants of man are never satisfied. Wants are insatiable. The very satisfying of wants leads to the discovery and even the creation of new and previously not recognized wants. Man being what he is, and the laws of life being what they are, scarcity will be with man so long as he inhabits this mundane sphere. That is why abundance must always lead man to greater abundance. Having realized abundance, man becomes dissatisfied with what he has and is, luxuries become commonplace and he seeks the greater abundance that broader vision enables him to project.

That which man can wisely ask is to have a fair opportunity, fair rules of the game, and that the quest for higher levels of living shall not be hopeless. We can seek to increase our productivity and the efficiency of our efforts for equitable distribution of the good things on earth, never forgetting that equity means inequality among men who are different in endowment, ability and in what they deserve. We must reconcile ourselves to the need of working and producing so long as there is life upon earth. It is in overcoming scarcity on constantly higher levels that we achieve the blessings ordained for us, develop our faculties and lift ourselves as human beings higher and higher above the mere creatures from which we evolved.

For the sake of brevity and simplicity, we can lay aside numerous concepts of value and say that economic value, or exchange value, has two roots, utility and scarcity. Utility arises from some quality inherent in the article and scarcity is due to the unsatisfied wants of prospective buyers. Both of these elements must be present before anything can have economic value, or value in exchange.

Value is not inherent in the thing to be exchanged, and may vary tremendously even while the thing itself remains unchanged.

Our practical problem is to measure that value. We inquire into its sources, course and relationships only to aid us in determining a fair measure for it. That is what we mean when we say that economics is concerned only with exchange value.

When something has utility and is scarce we esteem it sufficiently to exert ourselves or make some sacrifice in order to get it. The more highly we esteem something the more we are willing to do or give in order to get it; therefore our esteem is a measure of the exchange value.

Utility will vary with the qualities inherent in the thing which possesses utility. Thus, the ability of steel to cut through wood, and satisfy the want of someone who wishes to cut down a tree, make logs into lumber, or to carve a figure, is dependent upon the hardness of the steel. That hardness is inherent in the steel and makes possible the fine, hard edge which remains sharp as it cuts through the fibers of wood. But it may not be *too* hard or brittle, lest the edge break off as it bites into the wood or other substances on which it may be used.

For other uses the steel must be tough and resilient. There are many different kinds of steel, made deliberately to formula to qualify the steel for doing the kind of work which it is asked to do. The different qualities or attributes are inherent in the finished steel and determine its utility for one use or another.

As between any two articles or more which have utility for any given purpose, we will prefer that which has the greater or greatest utility, since it is best able to satisfy our want. But, this is only half of the "esteem" picture. We must also consider the importance of the want to be satisfied.

The importance of the want to be satisfied is outside of and independent of the utility of any article. The importance of the particular want to be satisfied depends upon two factors: first the number and relative importance of the wants themselves; and second, the number of units of the good available for satisfying those wants, which will determine which specific want of those yet not satisfied can be taken care of.

Among the most important wants is that for water. Among the many uses for water let us consider only four: drinking, cooking, washing and lawn sprinkling. If an individual had only one portion of water, enough to quench his thirst and no more, he would drink it, because drinking is the most important of the four uses to which he can put his water. So that particular unit of water would be more highly esteemed because it would be satisfying a very important want. If the individual had three units of water already, he would undoubtedly satisfy the three most important of the four possible wants. If now a fourth portion of water were made available to him, it would be esteemed less highly than any of the three previous portions, because it would be used to satisfy the fourth and least important among his wants for water.

Therefore, our esteem for a good depends upon the utility of that good and the importance of the want to be satisfied by it, which, in turn, depends upon the relative importance of our several wants for goods and units of any particular good, and the number of units already in our possession.

The utility which determines our esteem and which we use to measure the value of an article, is the utility required to satisfy the want next in order of importance to be filled. Thus, when we had no water at all the utility under consideration would be that necessary to satisfy our desire for quenching thirst, the most important of our four wants for water. If we already had one unit of water and a second were under consideration, the utility considered would be less, for it would be only that required to satisfy our desire for cooking, the second in importance of the four wants. And when three units were already possessed the utility used to determine our esteem and serve as a measure for the exchange value would be that necessary for sprinkling the lawn.

Since the utility which we use to measure the value is always at the edge or margin of satisfaction, we call it *marginal utility*. It is the marginal utility which is used in the measuring of value.

We must always deal with marginal utility because increasing availability of a good makes it possible to satisfy less and less important wants, and therefore utility diminishes as we increase the number of units available for use. Out of this fact grows what is often spoken of as the "law of diminishing utility." The law is that, under any given set of circumstances, the degree of desire for any good tends to diminish as the individual acquires or consumes successive units of the good.

What we have discussed in the above illustration is true of every other article or good which can be used to satisfy wants. And we not only consider the relative importance of successive uses for a single article, but also the relative importance of uses for different kinds of articles.

Water is important to us. But so is food, and clothing and shelter, as well as other articles used to satisfy a myriad of wants. In effect, but not too consciously, the consumer sets up a scale on relative importance of all his wants and then attempts to satisfy them in the order of importance that they appear to assume at any given moment.

But we must also consider the scale of wants of the person who relinquishes, or sells, the article whose utility is measured by the marginal want to be satisfied. The natural inclination of the seller, as well as that of the buyer, as a rational individual, is to seek those things whose marginal utility is high and to give in exchange for them, or to dispose of, those things whose marginal utility for him is relatively low. That is why both parties to an exchange profit by the transaction, the profit for each being the difference between the esteem placed on the utility acquired and that given up in exchange.

In actual transactions those who buy seek first the units which for them will have the greatest utility and then proceed to those which successively have less, until they reach a point where the utility is so low that they will not buy at all. In the same transactions, those who sell will dispose first of those units which have the least utility for them and proceed successively to those which have more and more, until they reach those which they will not dispose of for any price. So, while we have a law of diminishing utility for those who acquire or consume, we have the opposite, or a law of increasing utility, for those who sacrifice or sell.

The individual is both buyer and seller in any transaction. He acts as a seller with respect to the article which he is about to give up and as a buyer with respect to the article he is about to acquire. He yields a minimum of utility and seeks in exchange for it a maximum of utility. The difference between the two is profit. The same difference, if that given up be greater than that received, is a loss.

Thus far we have been dealing with esteem, or *subjective value,* value in the mind of the individual buying or selling. It explains *why* an article has value in exchange, and why some articles are esteemed more highly than others, but we still lack a precise statement of that value in exchange. It is only in the actual transaction that the several subjective values, or relative esteem in which they are held, are translated into exchange value, the actual quantity of one given for the actual quantity of the other.

It was in that way that the hunter and the fisherman determined the exchange value of rabbits and fish; and *the process is called bargaining.*

In a primitive economy which had not developed a medium of

exchange, and still depended upon barter for the exchange of goods, the problem of determining exchange values would be relatively simple because there would be so few goods to be exchanged. But, when production has developed and expanded to create a countless number and variety of goods, it becomes physically impossible even to think of the value of each good in terms of every other.

That is why a standard of value and a medium of exchange had to come into being before our present highly complex and productive economy could develop. We had to have a common language of value and express the countless exchange values in terms of a single commodity and unit. *For us that is the dollar.*

In England the unit of value became the pound sterling, in France the franc, in Germany the mark, in Italy the lire, and other nations had other units. But, in each case the unit consisted of a specific quantity of the commodity which served as the standard of value.

But the exchange value of an article is not determined by actually exchanging it for gold, especially now that the citizen of the United States is not permitted to own any monetary gold. The exchange value was determined by exchanging the article with other articles, and was then translated into terms of the gold dollar, or the various elements in the cost were added up in terms of the dollar and from the total cost could be estimated what should be the selling price in terms of dollars. A whole system of exchange values was built up out of actually exchanging or estimating articles with each other, which values were translated, by experience, into terms of whatever served as the standard of value.

The real service rendered by the standard of value in the determination of exchange values is to serve as an agency through which the economic values of commodities and services can be related to each other through a common terminology of value. *So, when we say that an article is worth ten dollars, what we actually mean is that it has the same economic value as any other article whose price is ten dollars.* For now we use a new term, price.

Price is exchange value (economic value) expressed in terms of money, as a specific number or fractions of the unit of value (dollar in U. S.).

To say that a rabbit is worth two fish is to express its exchange value in terms of fish. To say that a rabbit is worth one dollar is also to express the exchange value of the rabbit, but since it is expressed in terms of money (the unit of value) it *becomes a price*. And when we say that a fish is worth half a rabbit we have also expressed its exchange value, this time in terms of rabbits: but if we say the fish is worth half a dollar, or fifty cents, we have expressed its *price*.

So say that a rabbit is worth a dollar and the fish half a dollar is equivalent to saying that the rabbit is worth twice as much as a fish. So with all commodities and services. If we say that a fish is priced at fifty cents and we know that a rabbit is worth twice as much as a fish, we almost automatically say that the price of a rabbit is one dollar, since it is worth twice as much and therefore should be priced at twice as much. This illustration should help us to understand the enormous convenience of being able to express and compare the exchange values of an infinite number and variety of goods by merely comparing the number of dollars at which they are priced.

THE PRICE SYSTEM

From this point on we shall speak of all exchange value (economic value) *as price.*

The fact of prices, or a price system, is important, not only because it simplifies the comparison of values, but because it is through the price system that we must effect the distribution of the resources and production of the economy as a whole. Providing a common language in terms of a single vocabulary of values, it leads to easier exchange, greater production and higher standards of living. It is essential to the progress of civilization. But it serves a corollary purpose as well.

Having resulted from the production and distribution of goods, the price system in turn reacts upon its creators and becomes a means of influencing production and distribution.

For example, if prices are lowered on one commodity at the same time that they are raised on another, the effect normally will be to increase consumption and subsequently distribution and production of the article whose prices have been lowered, and exactly the opposite on the article whose prices have been raised. In this way the price system, with its changes and adjustments, tends to equalize the total demand and supply of commodities.

In affecting the distribution and production of commodities, price changes unavoidably affect the lives and fortunes of the human beings engaged in the processes of production and distribution. Employment can be increased or decreased, made more or less desirable, become more or less lucrative, all by the manipulation of prices. Whole industries can be promoted or destroyed, and even the trend of civilization itself changed, through the control and manipulation of prices.

THE DICTATOR'S DAGGER

Whoever controls the price system can influence and even control the very lives of millions of people. The possibilities of such a control stagger the imagination. The issue of freedom or slavery is inextricably involved with the issue of price control. *It is only when prices are the result of choices made by free individuals that freedom can be preserved.*

The one price system that is safe for freedom is a system in which prices are determined by the interactions of free choices, either in buying or selling, offering or withholding, of individuals in open markets. Nor should we let ourselves be deceived or misled into thinking that we can accept the loss of freedom in determining prices and still retain all other freedom. In order to enforce price control, it is necessary to qualify or destroy freedom of speech, assembly and all other freedoms, lest the mass of people refuse to abide by the fixed prices and insist on making their own price determinations through the interactions of their individual choices in buying and selling.

The formula or pattern through which these interactions of individual choices determine prices in the market, is sometimes called the *law of supply and demand.* It is an easy and convenient way of explaining price changes of all kinds, including wages, interest, rent and profits as well as prices of commodities, but does not and cannot explain the true causes of these changes. To reach these causes we must go back of the formula that: *"prices vary directly with the demand and inversely with the supply"* of goods, and see what it is that constitutes demand and supply and how they interact on each other and on the individuals who are back of both.

ELEMENTS OF SUPPLY AND DEMAND

The demand can be said to consist of the price estimates of the prospective buyers, and the supply consists of the price estimates of the prospective sellers. Put another way, the demand consists of the quantity of goods (total price) which the prospective buyers are willing to give in exchange for the goods they wish to buy; the supply consists of the number of goods that sellers are willing to give in exchange for the goods (total price) offered by the buyers. In each transaction, each individual party is both buyer and seller, as is apparent in barter. It is because we now use a medium of exchange (money) for which to sell our goods and which we use to buy other goods, that we find it necessary to use the apparently mutually exclusive terms of buyer and seller.

To illustrate the demand with two primitive men, a hunter and a fisherman: the hunter is willing to trade a rabbit for a fish, because he wants some fish and has more rabbits than he needs. He is the demander of fish. He would like to get four fish for one rabbit, and in no case will take less than one fish for one rabbit. The demand consists of one rabbit for fish.

The fisherman is willing to give up fish for some rabbit, and will gladly give one fish for one rabbit, but will in no case give more than four fish at the price of one rabbit. The supply is four fish for some rabbit.

But the demand of one rabbit is the maximum that the buyer will give for one fish, and the supply of four fish is the maximum that the seller will give for one rabbit. The actual price will be determined somewhere within the limits of one and four.

That is because there are other sellers (fishermen) who will gladly give more than one fish for a rabbit, and other buyers (hunters) who will willingly give a rabbit for less than four fish. So we must say that demand is the composite of the price estimates of the buyers and supply is the composite of the price estimates of the sellers. Somewhere between the maximum estimates the price will actually be fixed.*

Once we have the maximum estimates of what the buyers are willing to pay and minimum estimates of what the sellers are willing to accept, the process of actually determining the price somewhere between the two limits is one of bargaining. Each seller, knowing his cost, which is the minimum he can ordinarily accept and still stay

---

*For an excellent description of how this process is carried on, see W. H. Kiekhofer in "Economic Principles, Problems and Policies," (1936: pp. 476-495).

in business, tries to get more. The buyer, knowing the maximum he can pay, tries to buy for less. The composite of that effort among a number of buyers and sellers is called *competition*. The process of making offers, refusing or accepting or making counter offers, and then further refusal or acceptance or new offers, is *bargaining*. It goes on until a figure acceptable to both seller and buyer is reached. That becomes the price.

Theoretically, the price is fixed at the point where demand and supply are in equilibrium. That is to say, where they balance. If the price is fixed at or changed to a point above that figure, the effect is to bring more sellers into the market who will sell at the higher figure but would not sell at the price before raised. At the same time, the raising of the price above the point of equilibrium will take out a number of buyers, who would buy at the previous price but will not pay the higher price. Competition among the sellers will now tend to force the price down to a point where the number of buyers and sellers is again in equilibrium and the maximum number of exchanges can take place.

If the price were lowered from the point where demand and supply were in equilibrium, it would be competition among the buyers that would force the price back toward where it had been before the change was made. The process would be the converse of the first process in which the price had been raised, but would result in the same end, an equilibrium of buyers and sellers with a maximum number of exchanges taking place.

The force or urge back of this adjustment is part of what we can fairly call the profit motive. When the marginal utility of the good to be acquired is no more than the cost or marginal utility of the good to be given in exchange, there is no active effort to buy or sell. But as the prospective price rises above the marginal utility to the seller, he is increasingly willing and even anxious to sell, for the higher the price goes the greater will be his profit (the utility of what he gets over what he gives up). The effect on the buyer is exactly the opposite, although the principle is identical. The higher the price of an article goes the more utility the buyer will have to give up to get the utility of the article he wants to buy, and eventually he can make the exchange only at a loss. So he does not buy.

But, the buyers and sellers do not all get together in one huge market, as do those in a stock exchange or at an auction sale. In the ordinary and typical market a storekeeper places goods for sale on his shelves and counters. He does not know the subjective valuations of all his customers and he has to test them out with offerings at specific prices. He is likely to inform himself as to what other storekeepers, his competitors, are charging or asking for similar or identical goods, and he knows the prices at which he has been selling similar goods. So he sets a price at which he thinks the goods will sell and at the same time yield him the profit he needs or wants. If he is anxious to sell the goods quickly he will price them lower than the maximum he could get if he were willing to wait until enough customers with the higher marginal utilities for those goods came along. He knows that by lowering his prices, other things being equal, he will attract additional buyers for those goods or induce people who have been paying higher prices to his competitors to come and buy from him instead. If he has made a mistake and priced his goods too low they will sell quickly, but in that case he may suffer a loss instead of making a profit. Whatever happens, he will adjust his prices accordingly.

Of course, price is not the only factor. The public will consider the quality of the article, the way in which it is presented and offered, the cleanliness of the store, the service given customers and other factors. But, other things being equal, the reaction of the customer to the price set on the goods will tell the storekeeper whether he prices them too low, too high or just right.

Another factor which may delay reaction to price changes is habit or custom. People get into the habit of paying a certain price for certain goods, and they are ready to keep on paying the same prices, even though the cost may have gone down or up. For example: for many years milk sold at five cents a quart and bread for five cents a loaf, cigars for five cents each and street car rides for five cents. Even after the cost of flour and baking moved up, bakers continued to charge five cents a loaf for bread, taking smaller and smaller profits, until they either reduced the size of the loaf or had to charge more just to stay in business. Likewise with each of the other items. The same inertia asserted itself when the cost of production moved down and prices could have been lowered.

The difference between what the seller is willing to accept as a minimum and what the buyer is willing to pay as a maximum, con-

stitutes what can be called the "area of salesmanship or bargaining."
If either party is more astute, or better informed or more persuasive,
it is likely that that party will come close to his minimum in paying
or maximum in selling, at the expense of the other party to the transaction by taking a larger share of the bargaining area. This is particularly true when a very limited number of persons is concerned in
the transactions. But in a free market, such as a store on Main Street
where hundreds of people can buy or refuse to buy, as they please,
the price is likely to find its way very close to what the theorist calls
the point of equilibrium between demand and supply, or the point at
which the largest number of transactions can be effected.

In any country or economy in which the people have freedom of
choice, it is through interactions of their choices based on their
multitude of different marginal utilities for goods and the volume of
production of goods, that prices will finally be determined. The trend
will be constantly toward the point where the demand and supply of
any article are in equilibrium or where the largest number of exchanges can be made.

Prices so determined will in turn affect distribution and production,
for competition is likely to keep them constantly in process of adjustment. The conditions of demand and supply change with consumption
and production. No less important, the ideas of people change, and
with change in ideas come changes in attitudes toward goods as well
as toward desires and needs. Anything that affects our esteem for
goods must in one way or another affect values and in turn influence
the supply and demand for goods. This in turn affects price. So there
is an unending reaction among the forces and factors that enter into
the determination of prices.

It is important that these actions and reactions be the result of
choices voluntarily made by people free to make their own choices.
In that way the changes represent the composite will of the people
themselves and are in harmony with natural law, or the Will of God
as it is implemented in the affairs of men. Whenever anyone assumes
the responsibility of deliberately fixing prices, or controlling factors
which in turn determine prices, he is arrogating to himself powers
that belong to the Almighty or to the mass of individuals to whom
God has given freedom of choice and the responsibility that goes with
the gift of that freedom. This presents a goal not yet reached, but
worth striving for.

That is not to say that no man may ever exercise such powers. He may do it if the people delegate to him the power to do it. But, if he assumes the power, without the express authorization of the people voluntarily given, even though the consequences seem to justify the means taken, he has still violated the rights of fellow human beings. Experience has taught us, thus far, that the powers, when so taken, have not resulted in good for the community. But, that is another question.

INTERFERENCE WITH COMPETITION

There are three ways in which the normal process of price determination resulting from the interactions of choices made by free individuals (competition) can be interfered with or influenced. There are others, but these seem to be the most important.

One is governmental assumption of authority over prices and direct determination of what prices shall be. A second is monopoly, and the third is inflation.

Each of these three will be discussed more fully in later sections of this book, but at this point it is important to point out essential differences in the ways in which they affect prices.

Governmental authority, whether taken from or given by the people, affects prices directly. Some individual or individuals in government actually say what specific prices shall be and then, by power of the government, force sellers to sell at these prices and may even force buyers to pay no more or no less. Such a policy simply ignores demand and supply and the human forces which build up and constitute demand and supply. It requires more than ordinary governmental powers to make such a policy work.

Monopoly affects price through control of either the demand or the supply, increasing or withholding the actual number of units of a commodity or commodities placed for possible purchase by buyers, or those units which the holder of the monopoly will take off the hands of possible sellers. Monopoly cannot change the human forces which result in scales of values or bases of esteem for commodities, but it can influence the number of units available or demanded in the market and so influence the point at which demand and supply are in equilibrium.

Inflation does not change the human factors and forces which ultimately determine demand and supply and so determine price, and it can operate without even affecting the relations among the various commodities bought and sold in the market. What inflation does is to lower the value of the unit of value, to cheapen money and so raise the entire price structure. It multiplies the number of units of value horizontally and lessens the purchasing power of each. Consequently, it increases the number of units (dollars) which must be paid for the article which sold for a lower price before inflation. Instead of our rabbit being priced at one dollar and our fish at fifty cents, they may now be priced respectively at Two Dollars and at One Dollar. But the rabbit is still worth two fish.

So far as the relative value of commodities is concerned, inflation has little if any effect. But so far as the money income of individuals is concerned, the remuneration for personal services and from fixed income investments, inflation has immediate and marked effect. The salary or wages which an individual has been receiving now buys less than it could buy before inflation and there follows a series of growing and insistent demands for increase of wages and salaries so that the commodity income of the individual may remain the same. It is enormously important, therefore, that inflation be prevented, or, having been begun, be stopped.

In order to maintain a just relationship economically among individuals, it is essential that we have a stable standard of value and that the purchasing power of money in terms of the unit of value remain unchanged. That being true, price changes will truly reflect changes in demand and supply and the factors that enter into both. We shall then be able to deal more intelligently and fairly with situations resulting from those changes.

CHAPTER 4

DISTRIBUTION

a. The Problem of Distribution
b. The Distributive Shares
   Wages
   Payment for Use of Capital
   Interest
   Rent
   Profit
c. Summary

a. *The Problem of Distribution:*

Distribution has been defined as having two meanings: the geographical dissemination of goods as dealt with by the sales manager, and the apportionment of the total output of goods (commodities and services) among those who share in producing them. We are here concerned with that sharing of the total production through the distributive shares of wages, interest, rent and profits.

Since most products are the result of combining various elements or materials with each other and with human efforts, in the production of goods, it is practically impossible to divide the products of those combinings physically among all the persons who shared in producing them. Thus, a single Diesel locomotive is the product of hundreds, even thousands of workers. But the locomotive cannot be divided physically, and no one worker could be given the locomotive without depriving all the rest of their share of the product. Even with such an article as shoes, which are worn by all of the workers, the difficulty of physically dividing the product to pay each of the scores and hundreds of workers, is so great as to be practically impossible. And, even though it were possible to give each worker a certain number of pairs of shoes as his reward for helping to produce those shoes, that worker would still have the problem of disposing of the shoes in order to buy with them the other things he needed and wanted.

Another kind of production begins with a single product, or raw

93

material, such as a steer or cow, and consists of cutting it up into many parts to make it convenient for consumption. This is the converse of the previous kind of production, but it does not solve the problem. The animal is killed and then cut up into many parts, but even so, the parts cannot be uniform or so accurately divided that each worker could have exactly his fair share or what was agreed should be his share in remuneration. Then there would still be the owner of the steer and those who brought it to the slaughter house and helped in various ways to get the animal to the point of being cut up. No, in the final analysis, it would be just about as impractical to distribute the shares of a cow as those of a Diesel locomotive.

Fortunately, it is the satisfaction of wants with which we are concerned. And those wants, by their marginal utility required and the supply of any commodity available, determine the value or purchasing power of the commodity. If we can find some way to convert that purchasing power (power in exchange) into a medium which is universally acceptable, and can serve also as a storehouse of value until that value or purchasing power is wanted to put to use, and is also capable of being divided into such parts that any specific amount of value, large or small, can be transferred, we have found the solution to our problem of sharing the common product.

Instead of attempting to share the product itself, we can sell it and divide the proceeds of the sale, or the price received. This is made possible by the highly developed and universally acceptable medium of exchange, or money system, which has made possible the functioning of our complex economic structure. The product can be sold for money, and the money used to pay for materials and work done in making the common product.

Thus the shares received are in effect *payments for services* rendered in producing the common product. It is through these payments that we divide the product or distribute it among those who produced it. But before we discuss the problem of how to determine what those respective shares shall be, or how large shall be the respective payments, we must dispose of two fallacious ideas.

COST OF PRODUCTION THEORY OF VALUE

The first of the two fallacies is that the value of an article is determined and measured by the cost of producing it. That is to say that the actual investment, or amount of time, effort, material and tools used, constitutes in the aggregate the value of the article. If this were true hand-made bricks should be worth more than those produced by modern machinery. But it is not and cannot be true, since the price of an article, (exchange value in terms of money) is due to the esteem in which the article is held by the buyer and the seller. This has no causal relationship in the cost of production.

Instead, the cost of production serves as a limiting factor on whether or not and in what quantity an article is produced. The goal is the sale of the article at a price and the cost of production determines whether or not that goal can be reached at a profit to the producer, or at least without loss. Therefore, the value of an article is not measured or determined by the cost of its production. The cost of production represents what has to be paid for the several services and the materials and tools which contribute to the final production. And each of these payments, including wages, interest, rent, is an evaluation of the services of materials purchased, not of the article finally sold.

It can be argued, and with truth, that since the esteem of the manufactured article by the producer is dependent in large measure on the cost of the article, and therefore the cost is a determining influence on the seller's marginal utility, and so a determinant in price, we have already admitted such influence when we say that cost is a limiting factor as explained above. The important fact is that the causal factor is price rather than cost of production.

To illustrate, some years ago the author was advisor to a manufacturer who sold an article for $1.65 with a cost of about $1.25. His principal competitor was taking away the market from him with a comparable article, just as good, at a price of $1.25. My advice to the manufacturer was to accept the decision of the market, because that determined whether or not his article would be sold at all. He might not like it, but $1.25 was the market price, determined by the competitive factors in that market. He had the choice of meeting that price or dropping the article. So we started with $1.25 and worked back. After allowing a few pennies for profit, first, we made allowance for sales cost, overhead and the rest and came to a final 89 cents for manufacturing cost. The production manager did not determine the price of the article, but the price of the article determined how much could be allowed for the cost of production. The interesting fact is that the production manager succeeded in meeting the new cost limit, without reducing wages. The manufacturer went on and recaptured his lost market, at a wholesome profit on the total volume.

LABOR CONTENT THEORY OF VALUE

The socialist bases much of his case on what can be called the "labor content theory of value." It is his position that the value of an article is its labor content since *"As values, all commodities are only definite masses of congealed labour-time."* *

But Karl Marx was badly mistaken. And the many men, in the ranks of radicals and even among good labor men and the pseudo-intellectuals, who have accepted this seemingly sympathetic and friendly analysis of the importance of labor in production, have been badly misled and come to conclusions that make a fair and accurate understanding of economics impossible.

The truth is that people do not want things because a lot of labor is required to produce them and therefore measure the value of those things by the amount of labor in them, or that it took to produce them. Conversely, people do not hold an article in less esteem and become unwilling to pay a price for it merely because there is very little labor embodied in the article.

Quite the contrary: it is because people value the importance of the wants which the articles are made to satisfy, that they are willing to pay for the work necessary to produce those articles.

The labor content can be very low in an article that sells for a high price, or it can be great in an article that sell for a low price. Thus,

---

*Capital, by Karl Marx: translated by Samuel Moore and Edward Aveling, and edited by Frederick Engels: The Modern Library, p. 47 and 4: Marx says: ". . . that which determines the magnitude of the value of any article is the amount of labor socially necessary, or the labor-time socially necessary for its production. . . . Commodities, therefore, in which equal quantities of labor are embodied, or which can be produced in the same time, have the same value. The value of one commodity is to the value of any other, as the labour-time necessary for the production of the one is to that necessary for the production of the other. As values, all commodities are only definite masses of congealed labour-time." . . . In general, the greater the productiveness of labour, the less is the labour-time required for the production of an article, the less is the amount of labour crystallized in that article, and the less is its value; . . . the less the productiveness of labour, the greater is the labour-time required for the production of an article, and the greater is its value. The value of a commodity, therefore, varies directly as the quantity, and inversely as the productiveness, of the labour incorporated in it."

a hand-made stocking would require a great deal of labor, especially if made of fine silk, and its price would have to be high if the manufacture by hand was to be continued. Only a relatively small number of persons could afford to buy such stockings. Most people would not esteem the hand-made stockings highly enough to pay for the labor content in them. Now, if a machine were invented to take the place of most of the labor needed to weave the stockings, and thereby the labor content were very much reduced, the marginal utility of the stockings would remain much the same. Indeed, it might even go up because the superior quality and uniformity of the machine-made stockings made them more desirable. The reduction in labor content would not reduce the marginal utility of the stockings, but it would reduce their cost, and they could now be sold to many more people because the marginal utility of the stockings would be even greater than the marginal utility of the money which would have to be paid for them. They would be valued, not for their cost but for the service which they rendered.

An automobile made entirely by hand labor, using hand hammers instead of huge machinery to press out parts, would contain a tremendous amount of labor and labor time, but would be less valuable to the consumer than the more precise machine-made auto, and would possibly have to sell for even less, if it sold at all. The hand-made auto, with its high cost, would require a prohibitive price.

Labor time or labor content, like capital, material or tool content, is part of the cost of production and constitutes a limiting factor on the fact and quantity of production, but it is not the source or even an accurate measure of the value of a commodity. It is part of the distorted assumption of premises needed to justify a predetermined conclusion. Karl Marx needed the labor-content theory of value to justify the reasoning that led to his labor exploitation theory, but the fact remains that people do not value articles because they have labor content: what people do is to add labor content to materials because the finished article has value for satisfying wants.

RELATIVE SHARES IN THE PRODUCT

The problem of determining the relative shares of the common product which must be paid in wages, interest, rent and profits is not the same problem that we deal with in determining the price of commodities for sale, even though it is true that each of the shares is a price paid for services rendered and risks taken.

The elements in cost are not complete commodities whose value can be expressed by price in a merchandise market. It is only as part of the completed product that they have market value; and it is practically impossible to determine exactly how much of the total value (not price) of the completed product is due to any one of the cost elements.

Another difficulty in the way of determining the several shares in relation to the total price received for the product, is that the sharers are not actually partners in the operation. Some one person or group employs the others, takes the risks involved and hopes for profits. He becomes owner of the final product and, regardless of his success or failure in selling the product, he is expected to pay a fair price for the labor and other services used in production. And "fair wages" is as likely to be related to the cost of living, or the prices of other products, as to the cost of production or the price of the article whose total value is about to be distributed.

If the recipients of wages and interest, and the sellers of materials to be used in production, were willing and did share with the owners in the risks involved in making and selling, we would have a different basis for the determination of their shares. But the process would remain essentially the same.

There are limits within which the actual prices called wages, interest and rent are set. The difference between these limits, or the area between them constitutes the "bargaining area." How far the actual price goes toward either the upper or the lower limit will depend upon the relative bargaining power of the parties. The value of the product is determined in the market where it is sold (exchanged for other products through its sale for money). Then the total proceeds are apportioned among the several parties and groups who shared in its production, by the process of bargaining within the limits that set off the bargaining area. What are those limits?

There is a minimum limit for each factor. For labor the minimum is enough to provide bare subsistence. If labor is paid wages below the level of subsistence there will be a decline in the supply of labor and those workers still alive will be able to sell their work at higher prices (wages), thus forcing wages to go up.

The minimum limit for rent and interest is a payment that will replace the tools and equipment furnished and also pay barely enough to encourage people to save and to invest those savings in tools and equipment to be used for production. If less is paid there will be a decrease in supply of funds and equipment, and the supply remaining will be able to command higher prices or rates.

So with the materials and partly finished goods bought to be used in production. The price paid must be enough to enable the supplier to remain in business.

The same reasoning holds for profits, with this difference; in profits there is a payment for the use of tools which are bought with the moneys advanced or capital invested by the owners of the enterprise. But the largest part of the profit payment may have to be for the risk assumed by the investor or entrepreneur. If the profits are nil there will be no more investment in that enterprise or in competitive enterprise which might take its place. If the profits are too large, there is automatically an invitation issued to other enterprisers to enter that field and increase the supply of goods, with subsequent effects of lowering the prices and income to the enterprise.

We may state it as a general principle that the minimum paid for each element of cost must be large enough, barely, to sustain it actively as a contributing element in production. The maximum for any one of the elements is its own minimum plus all that is left after each of the others has received its minimum only. That is a way of saying that the most that any element in cost can get is all of the bargaining area between the total bare cost on the basis of subsistence and the net return from the sale of any article.

b. *The Distributive Shares:*

WAGES

Labor constitutes about 85%* of all cost and is the most important single element in the cost of production. In searching for a fair basis and measure of the reward or payment for the services of labor, we face an apparent paradox. In order to lift the standard of living for the workers we want high wages. But, in order to enable the workers to buy more of the things that constitute that higher

---

*To the labor cost computed in any finished article must be allocated the labor cost in materials and services purchased for use in production of that article.

level of living we want the prices of commodities to be low. So we have the interesting contradiction of raising wages without raising the costs of which wages are about 85%. And, even though we took away all of the payments to other factors in production we could not raise wages at a given level of productivity without increasing costs and consequent prices. The diminishing use of tools which would follow such a policy would lower the productivity of workers and make impossible the wages they were already receiving.

This problem is the more important when we realize that the entire economy is essentially a mechanism for exchanging the products of labor. To put it crudely, we all live by taking in each other's washing. The man who produces shoes, even though he sells those shoes for money, is really exchanging the shoes for bread and other things he needs for a living. So with all other workers. The real employer of the shoe-maker is not the management of the shoe factory. The real employer is the customer who buys the shoes, the other workers who pay for those shoes with the things which they produce and transfer in exchange for the shoes. Management is really the go-between which organizes the machinery and processes of production and exchange and justifies its remuneration by the greater efficiency which it contributes to those processes.

That at once establishes the truth that improved well-being for one group of workers who succeed in raising their wages for a given amount of work, that is, getting more money without turning out more product, is acquired at the expense of other workers who now have to give up more of their production in order to get a unit of the product whose cost and price have been raised by the higher wages without increased productivity. It makes it crystal clear that *it is only through increased productivity that we can have higher real wages**, and that the factor in production which has most to lose through exploitation by workers who have their wages (money wages) raised without increasing the output, is labor itself.

The round of wage increases which we experienced in the United States after the war ended in 1945, and through 1946, redounded temporarily to the benefit of the more strongly organized workers at the expense of the less strongly organized and those not organized

---

*Real wages equal the total quantity of goods that can be bought with the money wages, or nominal wages.

at all. It was one branch of labor exploiting other workers. And when the earlier groups of workers who had to pay higher prices for the goods whose prices had been raised, took their turn at getting *their* wages raised without increasing *their* output, they took back from the groups who had first exploited them their initial gains, and left all workers no better off than they had been before, some of them worse off to the extent of decline in production per man per hour.

We are told that the "laborer is worthy of his hire" (Luke 10:7) ; that we should not keep back by fraud the hire of laborers who have reaped down our fields (Jas. 5:4) ; and that we should do to others as we would that others should do unto us (Matth. 7:12). We are told elsewhere in Holy Writ that those who make use of their talents shall be rewarded with greater tasks for that they exercised their stewardship and yielded a profit, while the non-productive servant shall have taken away from him even that which he already has (Matth. 25:14-30) (Luke 19:12-26). There can be no doubt that labor should be rewarded according to its worth, in measure of its contribution. But what IS that worth? How shall we measure the contribution? What IS the hire of which the laborer is worthy?

We do not solve the problem by stating the principle. We still face the necessity of determining specific figures, and for that we must rely on bargaining. We can dispense with bargaining only if we are reconciled to foregoing the freedom of choice which IS freedom. Whether it be paternalism, beneficent or otherwise, or plain unadulterated dictatorship, or some form of collectivism in between, man loses freedom when his wages are determined by any other process than bargaining between his employer and himself. The same situation holds for prices of commodities and for each of the distributive shares in apportioning a common product.

WHO ARE THE WORKERS?

Let it be clear that the bargaining as well as the distribution is all among human beings. Capital as such receives nothing. It is the owners of tools or capital who bargain with other individuals for the shares they are to receive through the process of buying and selling.

It is easy for the socialists to say that all production should go to labor, and that interest, rent and profits are exploitation of labor. It is as futile as it is easy to say that labor produces everything. What we are talking about, and what the socialist misses, is that *wages are payment for different kinds of labor,* and that interest and rent and profits also are payments for the efforts of human beings engaged in production and exchange. Some men work with their hands and machinery, others supervise, some plan. Still others are engaged in transportation, or in financing, teaching, and the myriad of others in all manner of occupations. The people who receive interest and rent and profit have saved money and commodities and loan them to other people to use in production, or have risked their own savings in enterprise and manage as well as take the risks of loss. But all of them are human beings and it is necessary, somehow, to induce all of them to do their best in whatever capacity they may be working, and to arrive among themselves at what is acceptable and a fair distribution of the total production.

Nothing is completely produced until it is in the hands of the ultimate consumer. One may pick all the oranges in orange groves in Florida, Texas or California. He may own all the trees and the land. He may do all the planting and harvesting, all the packing and everything else that is necessary to deliver those oranges to the railroad for shipment to Illinois. But he has not done all the producing of those oranges and it is foolish to say that he is entitled to the total receipts for their sale. Everybody who had anything to do with taking or getting those oranges to Illinois, getting them into a store, selling and delivering them locally after their arrival, shared in the total production of the oranges.

It is not the labor of men who work in a factory that produces all the goods that come out of that factory. If there were no tools or machinery, that same labor, on the average through all industry, would produce less than 10% of the present production. Labor can well afford to forego demands on the small portion of the total product which goes to the tool owners and investors who finance enterprise and furnish many of the tools which enable workers to produce probably 20 times as much as they could produce without tools.

The productive capacity of a human being without tools or machinery, with only his own body and muscles, is about one-tenth of one horsepower. With the use of power-driven machinery available to him today, advanced technology and management, the productive capacity of the average worker in industry is more than 10 horsepower, at least one hundred times that of primitive man.

In terms of actual effort, labor can be credited with less than 10% of the total factory output, yet labor receives about 85% of the output. Tools and machinery produce about 90% but their owners get less than 10 per cent. The explanation for the discrepancy is not that labor is almost wholly productive, but that the tools are useless without labor and the otherwise generous profits would be followed by such an increase of competition among employers for the services of labor, as to transfer most of the profits to wages.

The end we seek for the productive process is the greatest good for the greatest number. Therefore the wages for labor must provide incentive as well as reward or payment. Greater total physical well-being must come from increased production per unit of time and effort of the worker.

While we cannot know exactly the share that should go to each worker in wages, the individual human beings whose remuneration constitutes the several cost elements, have by a process of bargaining, trial and error evaluations over the years, arrived at a working relationship. They have set up a series of ratios among the prices paid for different kinds of labor and other services of individuals in getting out the total product. These relationships, or ratios of exchange between work and pay, serve as the basis from which we can study and bargain further in order to determine more and more nearly accurately how much each element of cost deserves out of the total product, and, particularly, how much each should receive out of *additional productivity.*

But the resulting wage incentive plans, designed to reward increased production with increased pay, must be recognized for what they are, remuneration and incentive devices and not a means of distributing profits. Workers are not entitled to profits any more than investors are entitled to wages. Each should receive that to which he is entitled in consideration of what he does or contributes to earn it.

GUARANTEED WAGES

The personal relationships that exist in employment between master and servant in small enterprises changed when the servant, in a free society and growing country like America, became politically the equal of his master. As an employee he could leave the service of the employer for the alternative of cheap land or other opportunities in pioneer areas. The relationship became more and more that of buyer and seller of personal services, less and less that of master and servant.

Risks in employment were accepted and even welcomed, for they opened opportunities without exhausting alternatives. But the evolution from artisan and small plant industry to mass production, even as it gave us higher standards of living and comforts undreamed of in previous generations, also made workers increasingly dependent on pay rolls and subject to the consequences of decisions in the making of which they could not share.

Men have come to look less favorably on freedom with the looming promises of security. The certainty of wages begins to seem even more important than the amount of those wages. Workers are apparently less concerned over actually earning those wages.

Men want security, even while they have freedom, and, all too often, seem willing to give up some of the freedom in exchange for the sought security.*

The only real security for free men is rooted in the personal qualities with which they meet the situations of life. Out of individual self-discipline and self-direction comes the self-mastery which makes men strong. Men become powerful by accepting and overcoming the hazards of life. But it is only fair to recognize that there is a whole realm of hazards which grow out of the functioning of an economic order in which some men must make decisions which affect the lives and fortunes of many other men. These are hazards which workers cannot foresee and against which they cannot protect themselves as individuals. They may well dread these hazards, growing out of leadership in management, labor unions and even government, and they have a right to ask protection against them.

This has long been recognized by management, and numerous security plans have been tested by individual companies. For the most part, these plans have been aimed at stabilized production and sales so that payrolls could carry regular employment the year around.*

---

*The warning of Benjamin Franklin is not as widely known nor as seriously accepted by the mass of people as it should be. He warned us: "They that can give up essential liberty to obtain a little temporary safety deserve neither liberty nor safety."

*The writer studied such plans as early as 1919, in such plants as Joseph and Feiss in Cleveland, Ohio, and the Kendall enterprises in New England.

There was considerable progress in this direction during the nineteen twenties, when we experienced a post-war boom and good margins of profit. But with the depression which began in 1929 and carried through the thirties and to World War II, practically all of them were abandoned.

Following the Wagner Act and similar legislation came a tremendous spurt in the growth and power of organized labor. The economic security which legislation could not provide in the face of violated economic principles, was sought through guaranty of sustained employment. The method proposed by some labor leaders and welcomed by workers was the guaranteed annual wage at the responsibility of the employer. This would, in effect, force the employer to find some way of providing the means of payment of wages without regard for his ability to do so, or even his responsibility for doing so.

It is desirable, of course, to stabilize employment for the worker, and enable him to carry and fulfill commitments in raising a family. It is desirable for the worker and desirable for society, including the employer. We may not forget that your employees are the customers of my employees, and my employees are the customers of your employees, and if they are all kept employed, all enterprise is kept in operation. Likewise, if all enterprise is kept in operation, all employees are kept employed.

But it is another question as to whether the guaranty of practically full-time payrolls by management the year around will actually stabilize employment, as was promised union members by their less responsible leaders.

The experience of employers shows clearly that guaranteeing payrolls does not provide the means with which to meet those payrolls. Many plans initiated during the lush twenties died during the regression thirties. In some cases it was because the plans promised the impossible. In other plans, whose costs were adjusted to make them possible, the incentives proved inadequate to interest the workers.

A few of them survive in industries which manufacture consumer goods, for which there is a relatively consistent demand because of frequent and regular replacement. People are likely to use soap and eat food the year around, and in industries which provide soap and foods there is a possibility of providing regular employment. But people will cut off other expenditures such as fur coats, furniture, automobiles when buying power of their wages declines or ceases because of lay-offs or discharges from employment. They will make their old coats, furniture, automobiles and other durable goods serve them a little longer. A cake of soap is used up quickly and clothes as well as person must be washed in bad times as well as in good. A loaf of bread can be eaten only once and another must be provided, regularly, to take its place.

Therefore, the seeming success of guaranteed wages in a few concerns proves nothing with respect to other industries or even to other concerns in the same industry, except perhaps that it will not work in the other industries or other concerns in the same industry.

Even some labor leaders are now looking askance at guaranteed-wage plans. They are coming to realize that such a stabilization would require levelling, or at least averaging, of wages as well as production, and could well prevent successful demands for wage increases. Workers would have to share part of the burden of financing such plans, and the net result might be to weaken the hold of union leadership on the rank and file of labor.

Perhaps there is more nourishment for our would-be masters in just agitating without really solving the problem, thus further discrediting the industrial and business as well as union leadership, and hastening the day when a radical labor party takes over control of the government and assumes control over the entire economic structure. But the more intelligent, responsible and patriotic leaders among organized labor would not subscribe to such a program of dictatorship.

We still want stabilization of employment, sufficient to protect workers against the hazards over which they have no control. But we do not want to destroy freedom and individual initiative. Security may be comfortable, but it does not build a strong nation. Men decay under complete social security, and freedom is impossible without the errors and consequences of errors that grow out of less than complete knowledge and imperfect judgment. Man is not God!

There are three ways in which workers can be given greater stability of employment and protection against the hazards in our economic system.

First, the worker can save a part of his income every week during the prosperous periods to level up his income during the other periods. I remember a steel worker who came up to me after a lecture in Youngstown, Ohio, in 1940. He told me he was making $50.00 a week, which was good pay in 1940, but would gladly give it up and take instead a sure and regular income of $100.00 a month right through the year. I asked him why. He told me that he had a hard time getting along, even with his $50.00 a week because he would start buying something like a new refrigerator, or a washing machine, or some furniture, on time payments, and then he would get a 10 week lay-off and be unable to meet his time payments. He averaged about 40 weeks of work a year.

I was astonished. "You mean to tell me you'd rather be sure of $1,200 a year, working all the year around and getting no more than $100 every month, than to have $2,000 a year with 10 weeks off " And he replied, "You said it, Brother. I'd rather get $100 every month regular. The way it is now we use up the 50 every week and when the lay-off comes we're broke."

Obviously, although I am not sure that I convinced the man, the wise thing for him to do was to take his $50.00 every week while he could, but live on no more than $25.00 a week, as though his regular pay was $25.00 a week, and lay aside the remaining $25.00 a week in a savings account against the time when he was laid off. He would have to do that only for 12 weeks in order to have enough to carry him all through the year at $25.00 a week, slightly better than $1,200 a year, and he could still have a two week vacation with pay. If he followed the $25.00 a week plan right through the full forty weeks, he could save $700.00 for the future in addition to his regular living and twelve weeks of paid vacation.

Self-discipline and better budgeting would help many a worker to approximate a certain annual income. It is a simple rule. But, in addition to levelling off the peaks and valleys of income, every one should save part out of his income and put the money to work for him. That is the way thousands of self-disciplined workers have lifted themselves to comfortable living and comparative security in our country. Not every worker, by any means, has the pleasant possibility possessed by the steel worker to whom I talked in Youngstown in 1940, but everyone can save something. And such saving is one of the most important agencies needed to develop character and sustain a country of free men and women.

A second device for protection against the hazards of unemploy-

ment is to apply the principle of mutual insurance by spreading the
risks for some workers over all of the workers. That would mean a
deduction in pay from all to provide the necessary means to pay
the few during periods of unemployment. This is thoroughly feasible,
even though not easily popularized among organized workers. It
will accomplish the purpose, especially in the less violently fluctuating
industries which produce durable goods and even luxuries. Even among
the more difficult industries or concerns in industries where some
are already exhausting the elasticity of the industry in regularizing
employment for a very few of the concerns, this method can mitigate
the otherwise serious effects of fluctuating employment. There is real
merit in this insurance device and it is likely to prove an excellent
intermediate step toward realization of adequate protection for workers against the apparently ungovernable hazards.

However, it does not follow that the apparent success of some
concern in giving year around pay envelopes, without first deducting
insurance premiums from the pay envelopes, can be followed in the
rest of an industry. Whether the pay is deducted from envelopes to
pay each worker's share of the total insurance fund, or is not deducted, it is actually paid, either in lowered pay or increased productivity for the same pay. It cannot be had for nothing. In any case, the
pay must come from the income of the concern from sale of goods,
and costs must be held within bounds or the concern goes out of
business. *It is the worker who must ultimately pay for his own security.*

The ultimate and real security or remedy for the hazards in question is to mitigate the violent fluctuations in the business cycle. In
effect, this means regularizing production to anticipate demand. It
does not mean to remove or utterly stabilize all risks in enterprise.
Those risks cannot be removed entirely or even fully stabilized without destroying the consumer's freedom of choice which is finally
responsible for most of the risks and fluctuations in enterprise.

It does mean that business must undertake the responsibility of
reducing the violence of change and adjustment within business
itself. If the consumer and his habits of buying and living were the
sole cause of fluctuations, such a responsibility would be futile. But,
business itself, through the errors in fact and judgment of business
executives who determine the amount and kind of production, is an
important causal factor in consumer buying through influencing the

ability to buy. Business men can neither prevent nor remove consumer vagaries and eccentricities, but they can make adjustments to market conditions so frequently as to correct tensions and distortions in balance among the various industry productions, before they grow to the immensities which precipitate enforced liquidations and depression.

The fact that it has not been accomplished is no justification for failing to follow through on beginnings already made. Business men can do it through adequate understanding of the problem, increasing knowledge of the facts and then the self-discipline necessary to adopt sound policies and justifiable schedules of production.

The alternative is intervention by the state. It can be done by the state, but only through the limitation and finally the destruction of individual freedom. We cannot eat our cake and still have it, but we can acquire understanding and exercise self-control in the planning and supervision of our businesses.

To sum up: the annual wage can be paid finally only through self-regulation to stabilize business, with some help from spreading the risks of unemployment for the few over the many, and individual management of incomes and budget with personal savings out of every pay-check, against rainy days in the future. It is not a matter of guaranteeing the payment of wages regardless of production, sales and income, and so forcing the employer to find some means of providing the pay, but it is rather a matter of finding a way to MAKE IT POSSIBLE to pay the annual wage. It is regularization of operations that we must seek, and then there will be no need of guaranty at all. It is futile to guarantee payment of something which is not in the possession of the employer to pay.

b. *Payment for the Use of Capital or Tools:*

Since the Creator exacts no payments for the use of natural resources, either materials or forces, all of the proceeds of industry are finally divided among human beings, as part of the overall process of exchange of services for services, directly or through exchange of goods and money which result from the services. The reasons for and the nature and amounts of the payments differ in detail, but they are all paid to human beings.

The payments arising out of distribution of the proceeds of production fall into two broad classes, direct payments for the expenditure of human energy, and payment for the use of capital or loanable funds, or tools, which have been saved or fashioned out of savings for the further production of other goods. The payment for the first class, directly for the expenditure of human energy, is called "wages," and includes the minor classification frequently classified separately as "salaries." Both wages and salaries are payment for human services and belong in the broad classification called "wages."

The payment for the second group falls into three general classes: interest, rent and profits, all of which are payments for the use of capital.

INTEREST

It is only in comparatively recent times that the taking of payment for the use of capital has come to be approved by social usage and morals. In earlier days, especially before the productivity of capital developed and was so recognized, and when lending and borrowing were largely for the direct satisfaction of wants, such as for food, clothing and other consumer goods, payments for the use of capital in any form were called "usury" and were in disrepute. The transactions normally were loans and the payments were interest, but the differentiations made here had not yet developed and the payments were indiscriminately called "usury."

As tools came into greater and more diversified use, and as more and more savings were accumulated from the enlarged production of goods, it came to be seen that money borrowed for the purpose of procuring materials and labor for the producing of goods was in a different category than money borrowed for the immediate satisfaction of needs for food, clothing and shelter. The disrepute in which interest takers as a class were held came to be narrowed down against those who were greedy in the amount of their charges for the loans. And the word "usury," from meaning *any* interest charge, came to mean an "unconscionable" or "exorbitant" rate of interest, something in excess of the legal or fair rate of interest.

It was in the sense of exorbitant rate of interest that Martin Luther, early in the 16th century, used the word in exhorting emperors, kings, princes and lords to "rescue and save lands and people from the *usurer's* gullet."

With the gradual and then rapid development of industry, particularly with the enormous increase in production that came with the industrial revolution in the late 18th century, it became apparent that capital, when used to finance business ventures, could be reproduced and multiplied through increasing the productivity of labor.

Subterfuges used to justify earlier interest payments were dropped and it was frankly recognized that the lender was giving up the use of his own money when he loaned it to someone else for a business venture, and the money so loaned could become very productive in the hands of the borrower as well as in the hands of the lender. Hence the lender was morally entitled to compensation for the sacrifice made in relinquishing the use of his money. Out of this realization grew our modern theory that interest is payment to induce self-denial and saving and that the payment is made out of the increase in production made possible by use of those savings.

Today the world accepts payment for the use of capital as moral and legitimate, and points its displeasure and legal restrictions against those lenders who would charge an unfair or exorbitant rate of interest for the use of their money. This is especially true when the lender takes advantage of people who are unable to resist the exorbitant charges because of their great need and the absence of other alternatives.

WHY INTEREST CAN BE PAID

Without savings and the transformation of those savings into tools, mankind would still be living in caves as primitive savages, alternately glutting and starving and almost completely at the mercy of wild animals and the natural elements.

Interest, rent and dividends CAN be paid because capital, in the hands of man, DOES breed, the ancients to the contrary now notwithstanding, although not so clearly so then—and more than reproduces itself many times. To use a simple illustration: let us take a carpenter who owns the hand tools necessary for his trade, hammer, saw, ax, chisel and so on. He specializes in making window frames and doors for houses. But his output is limited to the number of boards he can trim and fit with his hand tools, and by the strength and endurance of his flesh-and-blood muscles. This is better than working with his bare hands, but still leaves much to be desired. He would like to do the work by machine, with power furnished through steam or electricity to turn the saw and smooth the boards, and so on, but he has not been able to save enough money to buy himself the necessary machinery.

Suppose he finds some other person who has refrained from using all of his income and has saved part of it in the form of money or loanable funds which others will accept in exchange for goods. If the carpenter borrows these funds he can buy the machinery and install the power plant needed to perform his carpenter operations. Now he is able to produce many more window frames and doors in the same period of time, since he is no longer limited in output by his own physical strength and endurance. His income from the sale of more windows and doors increases so much that he is able to pay back the money he borrowed, plus the interest paid for the use of the money, and now he owns the machinery he could not buy before, and has more money for himself than ever before.

It was the productivity of the machinery, multiplying the output, the capacity of capital thus employed to reproduce itself and more in the greater returns from his efforts, that enabled the carpenter to pay back the borrowed money as well as the interest he had to pay for its use.

WHY INTEREST MUST BE PAID

But, interest is not only paid because it CAN be paid. It is also *necessary to pay.* The mere fact that capital produces by multiplying the capacity of human labor to produce more, thus making it possible to pay interest, would not by itself bring about the actual payment for the use of capital. There are significant social as well as individual consequences of the fact and reason that the payment *must* be made.

Basic to all other reasons is the fact that it is human nature to value present satisfactions more highly than present contemplations of satisfactions to come in the future. Thus, suppose I am thirsty and have a glass of water with which to quench my thirst. You may also be thirsty and ask me for my glass of water, saying that you will give be a glass of water some time in the future when I am thirsty. But it is more important to me to satisfy my thirst *now* while I *am* thirsty, than to have the promise of a glass of water sometime in the future. It is likely that I shall be thirsty in the future, but this is *now* and I *am* thirsty. So you can have my glass of water now only if you pay me a premium or something additional as an inducement to give up the real and greater satisfaction now in exchange for the anticipated but not yet real satisfaction of tomorrow. In short, *I must be paid for waiting.* That is the economic motive.

You may say to me, "But you will let me have your glass of water now as a favor, or to be courteous or to do to someone else as you would have him do to you." If I give you the glass of water now, in response to any of those reasons, I am still being paid for waiting, the payment being the feeling of pleasure or virtue that comes to me in making a sacrifice for you. And I have even that satisfaction NOW.

In all uses for capital there is always the possibility that it may be lost, injured, partially or wholly destroyed, and the certainty that physical capital will deteriorate with time and use, and be only partially returned or returned not at all. Therefore, in addition to the necessity of inducing people to save, which is the genesis of all capital, *it is also necessary to compensate them for the risks taken in loaning funds or the actual goods for use, and the still greater risks involved in actual investment of the capital in enterprise.*

THE RATE OF INTEREST

Since interest is a consideration given in exchange for the use of loanable funds, or for control over economic goods and services, interest is a price, and that price is known as the *rate of interest.* It consists of an agreed-upon percentage of the amount loaned, paid at regular intervals, as a rule.

Being a price, the rate of interest is determined by the same process and in the same economic area that determines the prices of commodities or the price (wages) of labor. The process is the interaction of demand and supply, bargaining between present and prospective owners, or actual transactions in a market where the transactions are consummated. As a price it is also subject to arbitrary determination by government or monopoly.

DEMAND FOR LOANABLE FUNDS

The demand comes from persons who have wants to satisfy but not the means with which to satisfy them, and do not wish to wait until their own savings enable them to satisfy those wants. They may want consumer goods such as food and clothing, shelter, articles of convenience or even amusement. Or they may want raw materials or tools, or to hire labor, or all of them and more, in order to engage in some process or enterprise of production or distribution. And the quickest and most convenient way to secure all that they want is to buy it. Therefore they seek to borrow purchasing power, or control over economic goods, in the form of loanable funds, or money. How much they wish or will have to borrow will depend upon the nature and extent of their needs and also upon the benefits they expect to gain relative to the prices they have to pay.

The persons may be individuals or corporations or other forms of business enterprise. Ideally, a corporation or any other form of enterprise should grow and expand from income produced by itself, out of its earnings, surplus and savings. But those savings are often inadequate and the enterprise, initially as well as later, must borrow additional sums from other persons, businesses and banks.

SUPPLY OF LOANABLE FUNDS

The supply of loanable funds comes from persons who have saved. If they loan those funds to other persons, they must continue to wait, or forego certain want satisfactions, in addition to incurring the risks of relinquishing possession of their funds.

Since the amount of savings is limited a price must be paid for their use. If the risks involved are not great and the price, or rate of interest, offered is high, there will be a greater supply of loanable funds made available. More savers will then be willing to continue self-denials and take the risks incurred in relinquishing possession of their funds. The converse is also true. If the risk is great and the price, or rate of interest, is low, there will be fewer savers willing to relinquish possession of their savings. In any case, the rate which brings loanable funds into the market, or makes them available for borrowing, will depend upon the relative importance and magnitude of the risk and promised return to the prospective lender.

The supply of loanable funds comes also from corporate savings, from business concerns, or individuals having a supply of loanable funds in excess of their own immediate needs. Another source is the banks, which actually create loanable funds as explained in an earlier chapter. Finally, even government, through funds borrowed by itself, surplus funds resulting from taxation, or money created by government, can make advances or loans.

SETTING THE INTEREST RATE

No one can tell exactly where the interest rates will be fixed in a market. They depend upon actual borowing or lending transactions.

But we can determine approximately the area of bargaining or rate zone within which the actual rates will be set.

The upper limit of that bargaining area or zone will be the greatest return or amount of utility created through the most effectively productive use of funds by the borrower, or the amount of utility sacrificed or foregone by the lender of the funds. The lowest rate will be the least or marginal return from the least effective use of loanable funds by the borrower, or the least marginal satisfaction sacrificed or foregone by the lender.

These are the limits within which the borowers are willing to borrow and the savers are willing to lend. But the actual amount of funds transferred and the rates at which their use is consummated, will depend upon the number and intensity of borrowers and lenders, and the actual transactions which take place in the market.

The rate will be fixed theoretically, and in practice approximately, where the amount of loanable funds offered and demanded are in equilibrium. Above that rate, additional supply of funds will be offered and some demand will be withdrawn, thus tending to pull the rate of interest back down to where it had been. Below that rate, increasing demand and decreasing supply will tend to push the rate back up to where the borrowers and lenders are once more in equilibrium.

The rate of interest is both cause and effect. Normally and theoretically it should be the effect of interaction between demand and supply of loanable funds. But it can also be cause. Thus, an arbitrarily high rate of interest will be the cause which is followed by the effect of an increase in loanable funds offered to the market, or a decrease in demand, or both, followed in turn by a new effect in the form of a new rate. An arbitrarily low rate can also serve as a cause, followed by converse effects, bringing in additional demand and driving out some of the supply, and a higher rate of interest in consequence.

This fact can be and is utilized by government which controls or can influence a banking system, for the purpose of increasing or decreasing the volume of loanable funds in use or created by banks in the form of deposits secured by notes, by raising or lowering the rediscount rate charged by the Federal Reserve Bank to its member banks.

It is a delicate and can be a dangerous device to use, and it has not often been used either wisely or well. For example, in 1929 it was believed by many economists that the Federal Reserve Bank rate of rediscount (rate of interest to member banks on commercial notes already discounted by them for their own customers) should be raised to discourage undue borrowing for speculation. The Federal Reserve Bank tried feebly, but did not dare raise its rediscount rate in the face of opposition from business and industrial leaders who protested that raising the rate as high as was proposed would hurt business and terminate prosperity.

While there is risk in relinquishing possession of loanable funds through the making of loans, the risk is different and less than in relinquishing possession of any form of capital for whose use we pay rent or profit.

When the lender parts with loanable funds for interest, he receives a promise to pay back an equal amount of funds, which promise is protected by actual or implied pledge of other property in equal value to be forfeited by the borrower if he does not pay back what he owes when it comes due. This pledge may take the form of a note or mortgage. In cases where the actual physical goods, such as a horse, or a reaper, or what have you, are loaned for use, for which the compensation is called rent, the risk is similar in amount but not in kind. And where the compensation is to be profit, if there be any profit, the loanable funds are turned over to the enterprise as a permanent investment and possession by the enterprise, to be returned only as the business prospers and is able to pay, or if someone else buys out the share of the investor in the enterprise. The greatest risk in relinquishment usually comes with investment in ownership which entitles the investor to profits, when and if they are earned.

There are many problems leading to, associated with and growing out of interest. But, for the purpose of this study they are less important than the analysis here developed. It is vitally important to understand that interest is one of the three forms of payment for the use of capital, that it can be paid because capital is productive, that it must be paid to induce saving, capital formation, and that the rate of interest or price at which payment is made for the use of loanable funds, like any other price in an economy of free men, is determined by the actual transactions between borrowers (demand) and lenders (supply) in a market where people buy and sell or borrow and lend.

RENT

Rent is a complicated conception and a confusing term. It means different things to different people. The most common and simple conception of rent is a payment made by one person to another for the temporary use of a specific good or article which is to be returned to the owner when the time for which it has been borrowed has expired.

There is another use of the term which refers to the income or returns from land or natural resources used in production. Under this interpretation we become interested in the various uses to which land can be put, the consequent variations in productivity and in the prices that have to be paid for the use of it.

But, whether the borrower, or renter, buys the use of a horse to pull his express wagon or ten acres of land on which to grow beans or the use of a site on which to erect a building, he is dealing with capital goods which command a price for their use because they are or can be productive of other goods. This is easier to understand in the case of tools than in the case of land. A hammer is a hammer, even though there be considerable difference in quality among hammers. Their usefulness depends largely on the skill of the users. But, land which is lacking in fertility, or in the elements needed to grow into vegetables cannot yield what it does not have, and the utmost skill of the gardener cannot grow food in sterile soil. So the land does present some problems which are of less consequence or may even be absent in the use of other capital goods.

However, we must recognize land as a capital good, and even as a tool in production. The moment human energy is applied to raw land, or land in its natural state, whether it be to cut off the timber, or remove wild growth, to plow it under or level off its surface, or do anything else to make it more useful for the purposes the user had in mind for that land, it has become part of the total of capital goods. It is now a tool, the result of human energy applied to natural resources, the product of past industry used for the further production of goods, to be used for the further production of utility.

Land is like specific goods and tools and loanable funds—they all arise out of savings and are born ultimately of profit. What is important to us, in quest of a better understanding of economics as a basis for better and more effective living, is the fact that land falls into the great class of specific capital goods which can be used by their owners or by the borrowers of them for the further production of goods. They are specific capital goods available for use and must be returned when the agreed-upon time for their use has expired. For that use a price must be paid. And that price is called *rent*.

There is one outstanding difference between the capital for the use of which we pay interest and the capital for the use of which we pay rent. The capital that consists of loanable funds, the direct result of saving from monetary income, is loaned but is not specifically returned. That is, the actual dollars borrowed are not the same dollars that are returned. The borrower spends the money he borrows and later pays back the *same amount* or the equivalent of the borrowed dollars in other dollars. He may even pay back, with the approval of the lender, something else acceptable in lieu of the dollars borrowed.

But the capital that is made up of specific goods, machine tools, buildings, animals, improved land, etc., must specifically be returned, the same articles given back that were borrowed in the first place. The horse that you borrow from me is the same horse I expect you to return to me. Likewise, the factory building or the home I rent to you must be returned to me, just as you must return to me possession of the field which you rented for the purpose of growing beans or hay or other agricultural products.

And that means an additional charge for its use, because that specific good is subject to deterioration, loss and even destruction, which is not the case with loanable funds. So depreciation and maintenance must be added to the charge for borrowing the specific good, and the cost of rent is likely to be higher than that of interest for the same amount of value involved in the thing borrowed.

More important, loanable funds or the specific goods are used by human beings who borrow from other human beings and the physical differences among the things borrowed are of less consequence than the relations among the human beings. Those relations, in the case of goods rented, are subject to the same principles as those which enter into the transactions for loanable funds on which interest is paid.

Rent, like interest, can be paid because capital is productive.

Rent, like interest, must be paid to induce saving and to reimburse for the risks involved in loaning capital. The truth of that is not affected by the fact that the borrower of loanable funds uses those funds to buy tools on which there is depreciation just as there is in the case of a specific good which is borrowed for rent. The difference on this point is simply that in the case of tools bought with borrowed funds, the borrower of the funds takes the risks of depreciation and maintenance and pays for them out of his return, whereas in the borrowing of the specific goods, the borrower pays the lender for the depreciation and maintenance in addition to what would otherwise be a simple rate of interest, and keeps all of the return which he nets from his use of the capital left to him after the payment of rent.

The price we call rent, practically speaking, is determined by the same forces and facts that enter into the determination of that other price called the rate of interest.

Profit

Because the concept of profit is confused for many people there are serious errors in efforts to improve economic conditions. The concept is not simple because profit itself serves several purposes and can be approached from several points of view.

The basic concept of profit is that of a surplus above the cost of production. It consists of new utility, over and above the utility consumed in the process of production and replaced in the new product. For example, a man needs to exert himself to live even under primitive conditions. The direct result of his exertions is food for his body. To get the food he had to use up a certain amount of energy and consume some of the tissues of his body. If the food which resulted from his efforts was barely enough to replace what energy and tissue was used up in securing the food, there was no profit. The process just barely was self-sustaining, and the man could not grow or become stronger.

But if the process resulted in bringing more food than enough barely to sustain life in the man, then there was a profit, a profit by the amount of the surplus over his bare needs for subsistence, and the man could wax hearty and even use some of the surplus to exchange for other things he might want which were above mere subsistence.

Because he produced something which had more utility than was

possessed by the raw materials he used and the utilities he consumed
in the process of production, including what was necessary to keep
him alive, there was a profit, or surplus. And it was that profit
which became the genesis of civilization.

From that profit we produced tools and machinery, roads, bridges,
schools, churches, factories and all the rest of the magnificent picture we call modern civilization.

So in the parable of the talents, there was a profit in that two
of the servants not only returned what was earlier given them to
use, but used those talents so effectively as to produce or acquire for
their master more than the utility used in the process of employing
those talents. The surplus made each of them a profitable servant
who had used wisely his stewardship and brought back a profit as
evidence of the use.

In a typical modern enterprise we have tools and machinery, buildings, employed labor, materials and services purchased outside for
use in production, land or other borrowed capital goods, management in charge and investors or entrepreneurs taking responsibility
for the enterprise. There is produced an aggregate total income which
is paid out in the following shares:

> Materials and services purchased for use in production;
>
> Wages;
> Rent;
> Interest;
> Taxes;
> Profit.

In each of the above total shares of wages, interest and rent, there is
enough to restore what was consumed by the factors so rewarded
in the process of production, or what is required for bare subsistence, plus whatever is more than mere subsistence to bring the
total to the share paid. This "more" is a profit element, in that it
is part of the total surplus which the combined factors at work have
been able to get for themselves by the bargaining process. In this
sense there is an element of profit within what the accounting records
show as the "cost of production."

But such a differentiation within wages, interest and rent is not
shown in the cost records of the individual enterprise. Wages are
the actual amounts paid to labor, regardless of the elements included

in the wages. Interest and rent are each the actual amount paid, and then, when all the costs of production have been paid, there may still be something left. It is this residuum which is left that becomes the reward or payment for the risk-taker or entrepreneur who owns the enterprise and risks the capital with which it is run. This residuum is what we think of when the term "profit" ordinarily is used.

We have two apparently conflicting concepts of profit. But they are the same in principle, each consisting of a "more" that is left after the total cost of production, or the difference between income and outgo.

But, to avoid confusion, let us think of profit in the broad sense of utility created over and above the utility used or consumed in the process of production as the "social concept of profit." It is an undifferentiated total which in the aggregate consists of the total utility now existing in the world over and above the undeveloped resources that existed when man began his long march from mere subsistence to civilization.

The concept with which most of us are familiar is the "economic concept" of profit. This is the residuum that is left to the owners of a business from the gross receipts resulting from sales and other income, after deducting what they have paid or imputed for payment for the cost of materials and services from outside, wages, salaries, rents and interest including those on property or funds belonging to the business, replacements, taxes and related costs or expenditures.

This is computed in terms of money and includes what is left after all the expenses and costs of production, selling and administration have been paid. In the cost are included many charges for taxes. But the income taxes will be deducted from the profit and paid out of the profit.

As in the case of interest and rent, profit can be paid because capital is productive and it must be paid to compensate owners for the risks of investment in the business. If there were no profits there would be no investment in enterprise and production would eventually fall back to the low levels of making without tools.

It should also be stated that profits are the payment which must be made for the freedom of the customer in buying or refraining from buying specific products. It is by the exercise of this freedom of choice that the customer determines which enterprises shall survive or fail, prosper or not prosper. In effect his purchase is a vote for the enterprise whose product he buys, and profit is the price that society pays for the customer's privilege to "vote."

While the profit belongs to the owners of the business, it is not necessarily good practice to pay all of it to those owners. There is need to retain some of the profits as working capital and what can be called a "cushion" against unanticipated needs and costs. Wise management accumulates a surplus, as an accounting item, by retaining some of the profits in the business as a cushion and also for expansion.

The amount of profit is subject to debate, and much of the debate is based on misuse of the facts. For example, a mere comparison of dollars of profit between two periods, to show increase of profits as high or even exorbitant, is not a fair measure, any more than such a comparison of wages. Wages or profits may double in dollars, and yet represent no real increase in either, because the price level may have gone up more than either wages or profits and the purchasing power of the new wage or new profit is less than was the old in lower number of dollars but higher purchasing power.

In general, the portion of the national income going to profits decreases while the portion going to wages increases over a period of years. There was a time when the owners had control and were able to pay almost as little as they pleased, down to subsistence level for the workers, and could charge almost as much as they wished for the product. Now improving competition has made it increasingly difficult and even impossible to control prices, while, on the other hand, growing control over labor supply by the labor unions has made the risk-taker or entrepreneur the victim of costs he can no longer control. Squeezed between rising costs and competitive prices, the entrepreneur saves himself through superior and ever increasingly efficient management. If his management is inferior to that of his competitors he is likely to earn lower profits and may even be squeezed out of business.

c. *Summary:*

Profit is something created over and above what existed before the process of production began. The total product must be enough to reimburse the total expenses or outlays incurred in production and to replace the materials used, or the process will destroy itself. If the total product is more than enough to meet the outlays and replace the materials, the "more than enough" portion, or the surplus, becomes what is rightly called "profit." This is the seed from which new or enlarged enterprise springs, with resulting improvements in the standard of living for those engaged in production. This profit is the genesis of civilization, and is the prize which men in all walks of life struggle to possess.

While the total profit accumulated through the years in the physical evidences of civilization is included in what we call the "social concept of profit," we are more familiar and perhaps more directly concerned with what we call the "economic concept of profit." The latter is the residium after payment of all costs and expenses of running a business, which becomes the share of the owner in compensation for the risk he takes in investment. This profit is not only a reward for risk but also the inducement to other owners of capital to become risk-takers or entrepreneurs.

The encouragement of new risk-takers is tremendously important, for someone must take the initiative in every enterprise which serves to satisfy the wants of man. There must be a constant replenishment for those entrepreneurs who grow old or tired or too powerful unless there is active and adequate competition for their markets. Economic progress is not spontaneous in arising out of nothing, nor can it be. It is the composite resultant of many efforts in enterprise. To destroy the profit that motivates risk in enterprise means the ultimate destruction of civilization itself. There can be no expanding economy to meet the needs of growing population and rising standards of living unless there is profit.

Competition and fair play are adequate controls for profit among an enlightened people, and are a far more intelligent and dependable means than the dictatorial control of any group or interest. Indeed, the real problem in profit is not so much in the amount of the profit itself as it is the finding of ways and means to use the profit motive in the best interests of all men.

Profit is the most powerful of urges to man in the building of his living and lifting himself to higher levels of being, in subduing the earth and gaining dominion over its creatures, To be effective, the profit motive should be so harnessed as to make possible the greatest practical pull on enterprise creation or initiation and direction without discouraging the motive from which the pulling takes its inception. If the harness is made to fit like a perfect yoke, which leaves the limbs free to pull without hurt or pain on the shoulders to which the yoke is fastened, we can look forward to a maximum of benefit from the profit motive in economic life and, no less, an aid and encouragement to our moral and spiritual growth.

CHAPTER 5

CONTROL

CONTROL in economics is dominion with power to determine, regulate, limit, coordinate and supervise activities, relationships and rewards in the economic process . . . .

   a. The Problem
   b. Forms of Control
   c. Alternative Ideologies
 -d. The Collectivisms:
     Assumptions and Principles
     Socialism (The Cat that bore the Kittens)
     Communism (The Russian Kitten)
     Fascism   (The Italian Kitten)
     Nazism   (The German Kitten)
     Socialist-Labor (The English Kitten)
     Welfare State (The American Kitten)
   e. The Individualisms:
     Assumptions and Principles
     Anarchism (Voluntary Cooperation)
     Laissez-faire (Unrestricted self-interest)
     Democracy (Majority Rule without Restriction)
     Constitutional Republic (Government within limits provided by
        Constitution. Powers from people.)
   f. Conclusion

a. *The problem:*

In all activity, whether it be the life of an individual or the functioning of an organization, there must be *purpose, power and control.*

In our economic life, as part of our composite existence as human beings, there is the grand purpose of growth and development, self-realization through stewardship for the individual human being. This is another way of saying that the Creator is working through man in the evolution and realization of whatever was His purpose in creating man in the first place. We live that we may serve God.

125

The power that motivates our activity, that holds men to even difficult and unpleasant, but necessary tasks, that sparks individual initiative and the enterprises vital to our living, is the profit motive in its broad sense. As indicated in the previous chapter, it is our real task to find ways and means of using this motive in the best interests of all men.

Purpose can be defeated through the very efforts men exert in its behalf, unless the powers are coordinated and effectively directed in quest of the purpose. Working at cross purposes, ignorance of the consequences of specific acts or policies, misuse of powers, camouflaging the real purpose, and a host of other factors can operate to defeat the use of power to accomplish purpose. We must find the best method of control so that power can be applied wisely and directed effectively to accomplish our purpose.

The methods and means of control and the philosophy which directs both, can determine the way in which a society or group will function, as well as decide the fate of the individual in that society or group.

The absence of control is disorder. It is not, as many have thought, the essence of freedom. For freedom is not absence of restraint. It is a matter of who or what controls the individual. If the individual is controlled by himself, through his own volitions, he is free. If he is controlled from the outside, be it by individual or state, with no alternative or power of veto, he is not free.

What we seek and hope for through control is that method or form of domination which will permit and facilitate the most effective use of the factors in production. Just and incentive-provoking distribution will further encourage maximum utilization of natural resources and human energy. It is in this direction that we must seek the new frontiers of economic growth. The possibilities are enormous, offering greater rewards than the highest which man has yet achieved.

b. *Forms of Control:*

There has always been some form of control. The conflicting interests of individuals have always had to be reconciled and coordinated so that the individuals could live in contact with each other.

The most effective control thus far devised has been through accepted "rules of the game." Such controls developed from customs out of the needs and wants of individuals, actively pursued. Back of these practices and the philosophies which grew with them, has always been the religion by which man lives. Out of that religion springs his philosophy of life, followed by the choices or acts which result from efforts to satisfy his needs and wants. The choices or acts, repeated many times, became established in practices, and out of interplay those practices accepted by the group became customs. The customs in turn became the basis for man-made law or statutes.

The basic determinant is the religion which man accepts as the sanction and guide for his conduct, the God to Whom he bows as the Arbiter of what is right or wrong, good or bad. So it is that the religion of a people becomes the source of its laws. But, the tempo of change in development of civilization may become so rapid that customs cannot be formed in time to provide controls for conduct and a basis for statutory law. Then men establish laws first, through legislative action, laws designed to meet specific situations or problems rather than conform to previously established principles with their roots in religion. The people subject to those statutory laws then develop customs in accord with the laws, and make their choices in obedience to the law-created customs. Finally, they adapt their basic beliefs or philosophies of life, their religion if you please, to the choices they have already made.

So it is that we reverse the process which once began with religion and culminated in law, and which leads now towards the State as God and arbiter and final sanction, in place of the God of our fathers.

c. *Alternative Ideologies:*

There are two broad classifications or ideologies of control, the collectivisms and the individualisms; into either of which fall the various plans or schemes tried or proposed through the centuries of civilizing man. Between them there is unending conflict for the control of man and the determination of his destiny. It is a conflict that has waged since the cradle days of humanity.

The basic points at issue between the two groups are:

1. Who shall plan?
2. Who shall control?
3. Whom shall we worship?

The vital consideration in making our choice between the alternatives is: do we want freedom or security?

If we want freedom for the individual providing his own security, we make one set of choices. If we want security provided *for* the individual we must choose the alternate. We cannot choose both. If we fail to make our choice voluntarily the choice will be made for us, by default, or we may find ourselves in purposeless disorder and ultimate dictatorship.

The following chart is a crude representation of the alternatives and their results:

	Choice	
	Freedom through Individualism	*Security* through Collectivism
1. Who shall plan?	*The Enterpriser*	*The Government*
2. Who shall control?	*The Individual* through competition and co-operation.	*Men in Control* of government.
3. Whom shall we worship?	*God*	*The State* or the Dictator.
Ultimate result	Security through freedom and development of individual character and ability, expressed through individual initiative and enterprise.	Loss of freedom; the security of slavery,—through substitution of state will and force for individual responsibility and initiative.

Any one system or form of control may for a time combine the conflicting elements. For example, individual freedom may be lessened in the providing of state guaranteed security and both exist side by side. But what we must watch for always is the trend in one direction or another, for ultimately one of the alternatives must overcome and eliminate the other. And the resulting disaster or benefit becomes manifest long before the trend has been fully accomplished.

d. *The Collectivisms:*

ASSUMPTIONS AND PRINCIPLES

The basic assumption in the collectivisms is that the individual cannot be trusted to provide for himself and determine his own future. It is assumed that he must be taught, controlled, guided and made to do what is believed by those who control to be right and best for him. It is believed that only government can make men good, prosperous and happy. Government is the agency through which an individual may hope to make other individuals behave as he would like to see them behave, without interfering with his ideas of behavior for himself.

Therefore, the collectivists build their control on planning by government. It is axiomatic that there must be planning by someone to make exertions effective for any purposeful end; particularly when accomplishment of the end involves a number of persons among whom the functions and work are divided. But, the collectivist would have this planning done by the state as agency for the whole, which would mean planning by those men in control of government. And he has described the results so brightly and attractively that many sincere believers in individual rights and freedom have been led by the bait of "social planning for the good of all" into the trap of "state control and the ultimate destruction of individual freedom."

If the plans made by government are to be carried out, the government must have power to control the activities of all persons affected by the plan. The result is government by men who use the power of government to control other men; and we have division of all men into two classes, those who are governed and those who govern through the agency of the state.

The area of control includes the activities of men in pursuit of livelihood. The government, through its agencies, bureaus, or officials, must ultimately decide who should do what, where he should work, the compensation to be given him and the standard of living he may enjoy. This would necessitate that property, especially that used for production, must be controlled by the state; and the surest avenue to such control is state ownership. Under the ultimate collectivistic state planning for and controlling the lives of people, there can be no property or any individual responsibility other than to the state, or government.

No control of men can work unless men accept that control. They accept it only when they believe it is right, or the consequences of acceptance seem more desirable than the consequences of refusal. For the second alternative the choice may be in response to force or to bribe.

If men accept the control of collectivism because they believe it to be right, they have already reached the point at which they are ready to accept the state as arbiter of what is right or wrong, good or bad. And when the power to make those decisions is so accorded, the state has, in effect, taken the place of God in the conscious lives of those men. For men worship whatever power or authority they accept as the final judge of what is right or wrong, good or bad.

If men yield to the bribe, it is because the security and release from individual responsibility promised under government control seem more desirable than the freedom they lose. The very act of obeisance is a denial of the source of their freedom and constitutes acceptance of the State in place of God as the object of worship.

If men yield to force, but still believe the state control to be wrong, or consider the security offered by government less desirable than the freedom which it costs, they may yield for a time, but ultimately they will rebel and attain a renewal of their freedom and individual responsibility; unless they weary of the struggle and accept the bribe under diminishing protest. Ultimately they, too, come to believe that collectivism is right after all and their zest for freedom starves to death.

Ultimately, the control of collectivism can continue only if men come to believe in collectivism as right and best for them, preferring the bribe to the consideration which it costs, and finally suffer a deterioration in character which stifles even the will to protest.

We cannot escape the conclusion that collectivism leads ultimately toward deification of the State in place of God as the recipient of our obedience and worship.

SOCIALISM (THE CAT THAT BORE THE KITTENS)

Socialism is the parent of modern collectivisms, and as such is still the most powerful among them. There is a wide variance of belief and program among the adherents of socialism, as to the degree of socialization of property and centralization of control, the area and extent of government control, and the methods to be used in acquiring and using the control necessary to establish socialism.

There is agreement, however, on the two basic premises.

> 1. Recognizing that sovereignty cannot be separated from property, the socialist insists on collective ownership of the means of production, or of capital. Some go so far as to insist on ownership of all property, which would be part of

communism, but none deny the need of controlling the means of production.

2. Since the socialist denies private property in production goods, he must also oppose competition as the means of control. And his alternative to competition is central control in some form, to manage and guide production.

But he also believes in the levelling of income, so that he must concern himself with distribution. And, since taking over control by the state relieves the individuals under that control of planning and providing for themselves, the government or central power must also take over the planning of economic life for the group, with sufficient power to enforce the plans against objections from individuals within the group. . .

There is cooperation, but it is not the cooperation of individually free units, making their own choices. It is the compelled cooperation, or obedience to the State, necessary to make the centrally devised plans work successfully.

It is important to note that the socialist would not *destroy* tools or capital. He would still use them, machinery and all the modern technologies for production. He would do away with private or individual capitalists, on the farm, in industry or anywhere else, and place ownership and control of the means of production in the hands of the State.

The early socialists were called Utopians. Later there arose other groups called Christian Socialists. There were differences among them, some of which were Catholic and some Protestant, as there were also differences among the groups formed in Germany, France, England and later in America.

Some of the Christian Socialists believed in the socialization of all goods, others believed in individual property rights subject to social use of the property. The Utopians, generally, based their program of common ownership by the people in the hands of cooperative associations or the State on idealistic aspirations. The Christian Socialists endeavored to improve men and to implement Christian doctrine in economic life. They frequently pointed to the communistic experiments of the early Christians as the ideal for society.

Both movements have had their day and fallen into relative insignificance. They were mostly communists rather than socialists in the ordinary sense now accepted. But the socialism of today is associated largely with the teachings of Karl Marx. His "Kapital" is the source book of the modern collectivist, and his followers are more numerous than those of any other socialist writer.

Out of socialism have sprung Communism as practised in Russia, Fascism as in Italy (even though Mussolini was bitterly opposed to the socilaists in Italy), Nazism as in Germany, the Socialist-Labor State in England and the Welfare State in the United States. With all the variations and differences among them, all of them neverthe-less, in greater or less degree, have the essentials of socialism in common: these are the collective control or socialization of produc-tion goods, centralized planning and control, with the ultimate elimi-nation of competition and private enterprise.

They are all kittens of the same cat. The cat is socialism, with government control over economic life.

COMMUNISM (THE RUSSIAN KITTEN)

The instigators of Russian Communism, following overthrow of the Czar, were among the most ardent disciples of Karl Marx. They recognized and accepted:

1. The idea of the class struggle which must end with complete control and dictatorship in the name of the proletariat:

2. The revolutionary method, with complete destruction or isolation of all classes other than the proletariat:

3. That there can be no permanent peace with demo-cratic capitalism anywhere in the world. They are definitely committed to a program of world domination.

Communism as practised and in its program of world conquest is not only an economic system or theory of politics. It is a religion. The State in the hands of Stalin has taken the place of God as arbiter of what is right or wrong, good or bad. There is no appeal from that decision. (Not altered by the death of Stalin, March 5, 1953)

The dictatorship of the proletariat, as a necessary step to ultimate democracy, is defined by communist leaders themselves as the "most complete realization of leadership over all workers," the most de-cisive and revolutionary form of class struggle between the proletariat and the bourgeoisie, ending with complete replacement of all bourgeois leaders by communists even though the latter be utterly inexperienced and even unfit for the responsibilities undertaken.

The weapon of communism is force. All production and consumption goods are socialized by physical appropriation in the beginning. Equality of income is the rule, although not practised so far as the bureaucracy is concerned. Advantages in the standard of living, such as better housing or clothing or minor privileges, are used as bait to induce harder work and more effective performance in industry and trade. Freedom of speech and press and religion are freedom to agree with those in power, with unpleasant penalties for disagreement.

Control is implemented through soviets, or local councils of workers. These control life in the city and rural areas. The soviets in turn are federated into larger areas, comparable to districts, provinces or states, and finally into an All-Union Congress of Soviets, a huge body, too large to function effectively in legislation. It does provide wide-spread machinery for dissemination of orders from the top.

The real legislative work is done by a Central Executive Committee made up of delegates from the seven republics into which Russia was divided after the revolution of 1917. This committee is elected by the All-Union Congress and functions largely through two bodies chosen from its membership. Thus, on October 16, 1952, meeting in Moscow for the 19th Congress of the Communist Party, the Central Committee elected a Presidium of 25 members and 11 alternates, and a Secretariat of 10 members.

The Presidium is the top policy-making body. The Secretariat seems to be the top administrative body to carry out policies determined by the Presidium. The Secretariat appoints all key officials down through the bureaucracy.

It is significant that the name of Joseph Stalin headed the list of elected members on both committees, the Presidium and the Secretariat. Thus the Central Committee is ruled finally by the Dictator who also holds the office of Secretary of the central committee, and is a member of every important body in the government.

In all elections the voters are given only one ticket for which to vote. Orders and directives move from the top down to the local soviets.

Minor adjustments and concessions have been made in private property in consumption goods, and in religious worship while the second world war was being fought. Cooperatives are permitted and some forms of private enterprise are tolerated in a small way for favored individuals. Taxation has taken the form and place of seizure of physical products, especially from farmers, and the currency has been stabilized through an exchange of new rubles for old which enriched the bureaucracy and impoverished the rest. Foreign capital has not been encouraged except by way of gift to Russia, as illustrated in lend-lease help from the United States.

But the iron controls of production, distribution, education, press and speech have not been relaxed. In spite of the apparently highly democratic representation of the people and their apparent control over their own affairs through the local soviets and up through the higher bodies into which they converge, the Dictator is supreme. The so-called "Democratic Centralism" is an ingenious mockery, since the entire administration with enforcing executives and officials chosen and designated by the top bodies becomes an agency to disseminate and enforce the decrees of the Dictator.

The Russian kitten is now a full-grown cat, the self-fertilizing parent of communism over almost one-half of the world population. There can be no compromise with communism. If we fail to overcome it we shall eventually bow to its already determined world domination.

Fascism (The Italian kitten)

The core of Fascism is authority through the amalgamation of all classes, groups, interests and individuals as such into a unified will and responding to a single authority as spokesman for that will. The spokesman is now dead and his empire broken, but the ideas still live in part or in whole elsewhere in the world.

Fascism opposed Democracy with the charge that it denied quality with its insistence on quantity as a basis of measurement and political decision. Fascism built its structure on quality. Fascism asserted the "incurable and fruitful and beneficent inequality of men who cannot be levelled by any such mechanical device as universal suffrage" [1] It made clear that, "No individuals or groups, political parties, associations, economic unions, social classes are to exist apart from the state." [2] " . . . the individual exists only in so far as he is within the state and subjected to the requirements of the state and

---

[1] Benito Mussolini: The Doctrine of Fascism: Published by Vallecchi: p. 28.
[2] *Ibid*, p. 15.

. . . as civilization assumes aspects which grow more and more complicated, individual freedom becomes more and more restricted." [3]

Fascism opposed socialism because socialism "rejects unity within the state, obtained by fusion of all classes into a single ethical and economic reality, since it (socialism) sees in history nothing more than the class struggle." [4]

Fascism opposed trade unionism because such unionism becomes a "class weapon." [5]

Administratively, Fascism set up every branch of economic activity as a corporation or syndicate, with a council composed of representatives of employers, employees, technicians, consumers and government representatives to rule the industry or branch of economic activity. Each council had the power to rule industry somewhat after the fashion of the National Recovery Administration in the United States, except that the power in Italy was more extensive and complete.

The plan resembles one proposed by a C.I.O. leader who has advocated industrial councils made up of representatives of labor, management and government, with government holding the decisive vote and labor controlling the government through the ballot. The plan is fascistic and even incorporates a bit of communism. For that reason the proponent has been called a "red fascist."

The various branch councils under fascism were brought under a National Council of Corporations, headed by "Il Duce" or "the leader." Thus, the final word centered in a single individual who had at his command the all-governing body through which his orders were carried and enforced in all parts of the economic and political area.

Private property, even in production goods, was not destroyed. There was still private enterprise, but not freedom for the individual who conducted it. The State did not actually take over and own capital and the means of production, as happens under communism and is advocated by socialism, but did exert an iron control on the use of that property through the dictates of "Il Duce" at the top. All wills were fused into a single will, as exerted by "Il Duce," the dictator.

[3] *Ibid*, p. 55-56.
[4] *Ibid*, p. 15.
[5] *Ibid*, p. 15.

There was planning, and the authority necessary to enforce the plans, beginning with "Il Duce" and carried down through the corporate structure of the State. So the two principal attributes of collectivism were ensured through absolute control of production goods and centralization of power within the state. Indeed, these powers were centralized within a single individual who became the embodiment of the State.

The vital and what would finally have been the fatal battle for Fascism in Italy, was within the Catholic Church. Ultimately, the Church would have won its battle for God as against the State as the arbiter of right or wrong, good or bad.

Nazism (The German Kitten)

German Fascism, or Nazism as it was labeled, had its philosophical roots and pilot experiment in Italian Fascism, but changed the emphasis from the State as the entity to the race (Aryan) as the end purpose. Thus, while Mussolini exclaimed that the individual exists only so far as he is within the state and is part of the fused state, Hitler looked on the all-powerful state, not as an end, but as the means to a higher human culture as exemplified in his Germany, a "powerful weapon in the service of the great eternal struggle for existence" and ultimate triumph of a higher human culture in a race or nationality which possessed the essential ability for ruling the earth.

Administratively, the Fuehrer or leader (Hitler) came out at about the same place as Il Duce (Mussolini). His "National Socialist German Workers' Party" was organized as a device to win the masses to his cause. Hitler did not tolerate labor unions as such, but assembled them along with other forms of economic organization under one powerful state with himself as the leader, to direct, supervise and enforce the planning of the state for the people.

Here again, the essential attributes of collectivism were combined, in complete control of the means of production and the power to make and enforce plans by the centralized power within the state. As in the case of Fascism, it was not necessary for the state to take the risks of ownership. The state, both in Italy and in Germany, simply took control, by force when necessary, while the investors carried the risks.

SOCIALIST-LABOR STATE (THE ENGLISH KITTEN)

It began in England in 1883 with a small group of Socialists who called themselves the Fabian Society. They included some of the most brilliant minds of the day, such persons as George Bernard Shaw, Annie Besant, Sidney and Beatrice Webb, Ramsay MacDonald and leading lights among the clergy. It was Ramsay MacDonald, painstaking and impassioned, who more than any of the rest, laid the foundations of English Socialism and oriented the labor party into the arms of the Fabians.

They sought the same ultimate ends as sought by other collectivists, socialization of the means of production and highly centralized government with the power to plan and carry out plans for the entire nation, including equalization of income. But they differed in the method followed. Whereas Communism, Fascism and Nazism began with force, taking over the body of government and control of the country by force or coup d'etat, the Fabians were content to let Socialism creep into control.

They deliberately avoided the use of the word "socialism," but set out by advocating what was called a "welfare state," to be accomplished through economic reforms. They recognized that they had to overcome a strongly entrenched private enterprise system, the strongest in the world at that time and core of the greatest world empire of all time. They set out to overcome it by offering what seemed a perfectly innocent, highly beneficial, even Christian and certain long-overdue program of improving the condition of the workers by successive steps.

There was nothing said about total ownership of land and industry. Indeed, they saw sufficient for their purpose in state ownership of the great basic economic functions in a society, credit, power, transportation, mining. The rest of the system might well be left in the hands of private owners and still be controlled by government, as has been demonstrated in both Italy and Germany. For the machinery of control they decided to form a labor party which would later, in effect, become a socialist party under the labor name.

Whether or not they were aware of it, they had in prospect the absolute power once enjoyed by the Stuarts and other dynasties. When the Stuarts were expelled in 1688 and William and Mary of Orange were placed on the throne, the absolute power of the

Stuarts was not destroyed. It was simply transferred to the Parliament, which then became the absolute power in England, and still has that power.

The Fabians succeeded. Bit by bit they introduced what was later comparable to the New Deal measures in the United States. That staunch old Liberal statesman, Lloyd George, taken in along with the rest of the Liberal Party, helped put over the measures sought by the Fabians and then, too late, recognized the consequences of the program he was using to win the votes of the masses. He saw how he and others had been used to build a labor party to take the place of the Liberals and set the stage for full-blown socialism. To quote a contemporary English writer "there was no need for the Socialists to wait for the revolution. The realization of socialism had begun from the moment when the State became accessible to social reform ideas." Social reformers, having little or no idea of what socialism was or meant, became in effect proponents for a socialistic state in England. They strove consciously for reforms, but in so doing helped also to establish centralized power in government, and established at last the two cardinal requirements of a collectivistic state, planning and control by government.

So, under the guise of social reform and through the machinery of the labor party, socialism has been established in England, with a declining standard of living and gradually disappearing likelihood of ever reestablishing the once great empire on which the sun never set. In place of the once powerful essentially private enterprise economy we have now the socialistic-labor state which would have passed out some time ago, but for aid from the United States. We financed the establishment of socialist labor control and certainly its survival after 1945.

Even the election of the Winston Churchill government was a doubtful antidote for the socialist state already built. It is by no means certain that Mr. Churchill and his party will remain in power and it already seems apparent that the collectivist economy omelet has gone too far to be unscrambled.

By a different route, minus the bloodshed and terrorism that was experienced in Russia, Italy and Germany, but no less certainly, England has established the controls that constitute the essentials of collectivism. Socialism is a parasitic economy on a capitalistic base and it must go on to complete totalitarianism or to failure as an economic system. It is the half-way house to communism.

THE WELFARE-STATE (THE AMERICAN KITTEN)

Millions of Americans do not realize that Socialism is just as great a menace to freedom under any other name as it is under its proper label. Whether it is called social reform, the New Deal, the Fair Deal, the Welfare State, or by any other name, and regardless of the benefits that may be effected through its measures, the real danger lies in its elimination of competition, equalization of income, planning and control by government of our economic machinery and life.

Nor dare we console ourselves with the false comfort that there are not enough socialists and certainly not enough communists to win an election and take over the necessary controls.

England was taken over by a society which, in its palmiest days, never exceeded one hundredth of one percent of the population. Both the socialist and communist parties in the United States are stronger than that. It is estimated that the communists and their fellow-travellers alone number more than 400,000, one hundred times as many as the maximum membership of the English Fabians. They win, not by their numbers, but by having their ideas accepted by other groups, who thereby become fellow-travellers without always knowing it. Just as the Fabians relied on penetration and capture of agencies of public opinion and information, so our own leftists, both socialist and communist, have wormed their way into positions of growing and already great influence over schools and churches. It was not without truth that Earl Browder boasted some time ago that the Communist Party had succeeded in establishing a common front with many of the Churches of America· and, more than any other group, had succeeded in bringing their non-religious ideas into acceptance by the religious masses of America.

Here, as in England, the collectivists began with a welfare program. They aroused tremendous interest and support among the very people who had most to lose in a collectivistic society, business groups as well as church and school. It has been said that even England has not gone as far down the road toward totalitarianism as has the United States in the number and variety of welfare measures already in effect, and the concentration of power in the chief excutive.

No sensible person would deny protection against the hazards of unemployment and all that goes with it, but it is the *method* of securing the improvements that leads to their ultimate futility. For the method used by politicians in America is close to that of the politicians in England; assumption of responsibility by the government for individual and specific welfare of the citizen, with the power and measure of control necessary to meet that responsibility. Once that method is initiated it is only a question of time before socialism is a fact and then starts off on the rest of the journey toward the totalitarian state and the substituion of the State for God.

Such a government does not need to *own* the means of production. It needs only to control them, whether it be through credit and bank control, price control, licensing of business by the Federal Government, international treaties which supercede our Constitution or other devices to bring our economic life under control of the central government.

Our welfare program has already taken us dangerously far down the road to socialism. The agencies or instruments of power which Franklin D. Roosevelt once said had been built up in his time and which he characterized as "dangerous in other hands" than his own, did fall into other hands. Harry Truman carried socialism even further than did Roosevelt. He piled up the national debt by the greatest spending orgy in our history, increased greatly the extent and functions of the bureaucracy, stimulated inflation with the futility of his controls and assumed unto himself powers which Mr. Roosevelt had not dared to take. Whereas Roosevelt maintained the forms of a Republic while he built within them the foundations of empire, Truman gave unmistakable evidence of getting ready to emulate the late Julius Caesar in lifting the crown to his brow.

Since then there has been a distinct revulsion against Harry Truman and his administration. Charges of corruption, only too frequently sustained in fact, communist infiltration into high places in government, executive indifference and even resentment against warnings by both friend and foe, the unpopular war in Korea begun with outrageous unconstitutional assumption of Congressional prerogative and responsibility by Mr. Truman, and other factors combined to defeat him and his candidate by the largest popular vote and majority in the history of our country.

General Dwight Eisenhower has since become President of the United States with a working majority, although slim, in both houses of the Congress. The warring elements within the Republican Party apparently have reconciled differences sufficiently to give the new President the support he needs. From important sections of the Democratic Party in Congress will undoubtedly come support for some of the measures of the new administration. Cabinet selections were hailed generally as promising efficiency and honesty, and there is growing realization of the special ability of the new President in dealing with and organizing men to carry out tasks compositely determined.

In the judgment of the author the election of Dwight Eisenhower, early steps in his administration and his already evident indisposition to emulate Harry Truman's ideas of personal power promise well for the American people. We have been given a reprieve from the vaunting welfare state.

But it would be a mistake to delude ourselves with the belief that the election of November 4, 1952, giving us a Republican President and Congress solves our problems. Even President Eisenhower is going to recognize the desires and aims of the American people, and the real danger of socialism still exists. Indeed, the danger may be greater than before because of our growing complacency and sense of security, giving greater encouragement to the ideals and aspirations of a generation which came to physical maturity under the New Deal and its successor. The great task of renewing faith in the objectives and basic principles of the Founding Fathers of our nation is still with us. We dare not relax our efforts to correct the socialistic trends that had their nurturing in the Welfare State inaugurated by the two previous administrations. Whether or not our economic and political omelet has gone past the point of unscrambling is still to be seen.

e. *The Individualisms:*

Whereas the collectivists begin with the assumption that individual man is unable to provide for himself and his future, and that his rights and liberties come from government, without which he can have neither, the ideologies of individualism are based on the assumption that man gets his rights from God, with freedom as an "inherent right," and that it is more important to develop the individual on the level of self-reliance than to provide for him that which he is deemed unable to secure for himself.

The collectivists, following Plato, would think in terms of the state and set up a permanent bureaucracy, as a privileged group, with the responsibility and power to plan and provide for those whom the bureaucracy governs. The individualists would think in terms of the individual and recognize the supreme importance of developing self-motivated and self-reliant individual human beings; to be accomplished through the exercise of individual powers and self-government.

Hence the collectivists establish "government by men," using the machinery of government to control the lives and destinies of other men, with a resulting cleavage into the governed and the governing. But the individualists establish "government by law," with government limited to certain powers and itself subject to the same basic laws that protect the citizen in his inherent rights.

Under individualism forms of government the state is the servant of the people instead of the master. Responsibility for conduct runs from the individual to his God for standards of what is right or wrong, good or bad, rather than to a government which furnishes standards for the people. In one case government takes its cue for morals from the religion of the people. In the other case the government sets up the standards and provides the religion for the people.

Under individualism improvement of society is sought through improving the individual who, in the aggregate, constitutes society, rather than building a strong state and system under which men can be made to do what it is believed that they should do. The individual is encouraged to make his own choices, based on his personal code of conduct, but within the laws which protect every individual in that exercise.

Government is primarily a means of maintaining order, national defense and internal conditions under which individuals can exercise their freedom without destroying that of other citizens. It was through such a government that Jefferson saw the possibility of training citizens to govern themselves and make themselves fit for freedom.

There are three categories of individualism government.

ANARCHISM

I do not include anarchism as a form of control, because under anarchism there is no control whatever outside of the individual. Government is abolished, the individual and the individual only is of consequence. This does not mean disorder and riot, as the word "anarchy" is ordinarily used to describe, but rather voluntary cooperation among men who are so nearly perfect that no government is necessary. Private property would be abolished, so men could be free of competitive struggle and incentives to quarrel with each other. There would be no wars and no need of government or authority to gather one group against another.

Anarchism is a beautiful ideal, for it assumes perfect humanity, with complete understanding, complete obedience to God and His laws, and uninterrupted prosperity. Education is the means through which the beautiful ideals are to be accomplished. But it is an impossible system with human beings constituted as they now are. And we must begin with man as he is.

LAISSEZ-FAIRE

Laissez-faire means absence of restraint on the individual. The need of government is recognized, but for no more than what is barely needed to protect life, liberty and property. The individual is trusted to do what is right and best through seeking his highest self-interest as he sees it. With each individual following that course, it is believed that the best interests of all will be served.

Free competition without any governmental interference is considered adequate as the means of social control and the surest way to a perfect economic system. By letting men alone, such government as does exist will promote the highest degree of social welfare.

Much of the early thinking in the United States was along these lines, and in sympathy with the philosophy of natural rights of man. In the beginning, and for a short time, laissez-faire played an important part in developing initiative and resourcefulness and successful enterprise among citizens of the rapidly-growing nation which emerged from the war with England. But, as time went on, and the economic structure and its problems became more complex and interdependent, the young nation learned to introduce regulations beyond mere policing measures in order to protect the very freedom we fought for in the beginning. Laissez-faire is not adequate for a society of modern needs and opportunities, and it is a mistake to characterize our economic system for the past century and a half as a laissez-faire system. It has never been truly that.

PURE DEMOCRACY

A second form of control is democracy in its pure form. Democracy is a much abused word and its meaning anything but clear to most people. For purposes of clarity let me point out the essential characteristics of a pure democracy, as the power of the majority to rule. In a democracy in the true sense, the majority has all power. There is government, theoretically the servant of the people and representing the people, as elected by the majority. There is private enterprise and private property, planning by those who are responsible for carrying on the activities for which the planning is done, as must be true of all individualisms. But the terrible weakness and danger in pure democracy is the fact that the majority can pass or set up and enforce what laws they please, and leave the minority with no recourse except to make converts out of the present majority in order to transform the present minority into the majority of tomorrow.

This weakness has invariably led to the downfall of the democracy in pure form. The result is tyranny by the majority and then some powerful individual rises to control the majority and collectivism is on its way in. Ultimately, the system winds up with an absolute monarch or dictator.

CONSTITUTIONAL REPUBLIC

The most successful form of individualism as a political and economic system is what can be called the "Constitutional Republic," the system developed in the United States. It is far from perfect but comes closer to realizing our purpose through what powers are at our disposal, than any other system yet known to man.

Like laissez-faire, it lays great emphasis on the individual, recognizes private property and individual initiative spurred by hope of profit and fear of loss, and the idea of a minimum of government necessary to maintain conditions under which the individual can do his best. But there is a difference on what constitutes that minimum of government. Under laissez-faire it IS a minimum, but under the constitutional republic there is recognition of the need for regulation in the public interest and for laws to keep competition fair.

The great strength of the constitutional republic lies in the fact that a written constitution protects even a single individual from encroachment on individual rights; the majority and even the government itself have to bow before that basic law in the Constitution. The limits within which men can exercise their initiative are adequate although not unlimited, and men are given sufficient incentive to exercise their capacities to the utmost.

All the machinery needed for national defense is provided for in that same constitution, and the individual is protected in the ownership of his property and his right of contract.

The great safeguard in the system is the arrangement of checks and balances which divides the power and responsibility among the several branches of government so as to protect the citizen against abuse of power in any of the branches. The protection is as real as the integrity of the Supreme Court which reviews the constitutionality of acts and laws and can reverse any act or law which it finds in violation of the constitutional guarantees. Appointment to the Supreme Court is for life and for success of the system it is imperative to have a court composed of the ablest and most statesmanlike of our judges, men above the level of political bias and out of reach of political influence.

There is weakness in the system, due to inadequate understanding and ability among those whose voluntary cooperation we need as the means of social control; education has fallen far short of what is needed to develop fitness for freedom. But the answer is not to do away with the protection and guarantees provided by that Constitution. There is adequate provision for important adjustments in the Constitution, and the provisions are not dangerous except as they may be used by a people grown weary of the disciplines of freedom, the work and vigilance necessary to protect our liberty.

Just as under other individualisms, the planning is done by the individuals who are responsible for carrying on of the economic process; control is through individuals enforcing the laws to which state and individual alike must bow. The consequence is that freedom is finally preserved through continuing faith in and obedience to God.

f. *Conclusion:*

The real control under an individualism must be developed in self-control of the individual under laws which in turn have their ultimate sanction in the religion of the people and recognition of the Creator as Lord over All.

It is true that in recent years, for almost a generation, insidious encroachments have brought subtle changes in our Constitutional Republic. Our rights as individuals have been compromised, some of them by the very government officials who swear allegiance to the Constitution in taking office. Government has been endowed with or permitted to exercise powers detrimental to individual freedom. The great danger persists and grows greater as we yield to government more power to control the economic life of the nation. The danger is further magnified in permitting government to plan for the people, and so relieve individuals of the responsibilities and functions which are needed for their development and which they dare not relinquish if they are to achieve fulfilment as individual human beings. Government provision for specific and individual welfare, misapplied under the general welfare clause of the Constitution, begins to demoralize the self-reliance and spiritual stamina of the people. We suffer from creeping socialism, the bit by bit substitution of the state for the individual in responsibility for individuals.

We must restore faith in God, in freedom and in the capacity of men to become fit for freedom.

PART THREE - FALLACY IN FAITH AND FACT

CHAPTER 1

SPASMS OF THE ISMS

ONE pities the poor savage who trusted implicity in the idol
he had helped carve out of wood or stone and who hurled
the curses of that god at his rifle-bearing enemy even as the bullet
crashed through his breast and laid him low. Poor wretch! Civilization had not yet revealed to him the True God!

How superior we are who know the True God, the God who
listens to our supplications and points the way to superior destiny.
So a sword-waving Teuton stood on the balcony of his house and
shouted to the multitude below, "With God, for King and Country!"
You see, he had an inside track: the Eternal God was at his side,
standing by him as he drove his enemies back!

And those same enemies prayed to the same God, confident that
He would give their cause the victory against the sword-waving
Teuton. Still others invoked their One True God under the banner
of another prophet, a prophet who had explained to them that they
were the only true believers and would wipe the earth free of the
unbelievers.

So, from one part of the world to another, in one age after
another, girding for conflict to win spoils and booty, or gathering
strength to make their power prevail, nations of men and women
have lifted their symbols of religion in somewhat the same fashion
that an army raises its banners, to march with some man-conceived
God in their van.

We view the spectacle of those poor, misguided fanatics, and
give thanks that we are not as they. We are grateful, who are so
much better off, for the blessings of the True God, for our higher
understanding of Him and His works.

Within our own borders are those who tell us that God has pre-
ordained our fate. Even before we came into the world, we are told,
it was written what we would be and what would happen to us.
Another group, with fine earnestness, tells us that we can be saved
only by His grace, and, once saved, we can never be lost again. That
is the special dispensation of God to them, His loyal and chosen

children. Still another group tremble at the very thought of the poor souls who have not come to them for the true formula to approach the Throne. But, even as their souls bleed for the poor unshriven sinners outside, they refuse to associate too intimately with the rest, lest their faith become diluted through the contact.

Each of these, and many others, has his own God, just a little different in that He is the True God and they have the proper approach. One is impelled to cry out: so many gods, so many creeds, so many paths that wind and wind, when what this world of ours needs, is just the art of being kind.

Above us all, somewhere, is the Eternal looking down on the spectacle of human gnats telling each other who and what He is, how He works, what He expects, each of them with his fellow-motes dragging a little set of harness with which to hitch God to his kiddie-car.

But we do go to Church, don't we? And under the spell of the preacher's eloquence we are lifted up above and beyond ourselves. Almost we are persuaded really to believe; under the spell of the music we may even dedicate ourselves to the beautiful, intangible ideals held up for us. And with the final Amen we may walk out of the building in a spiritual aura, until we hit the solid fact of air and a practical world awaiting us beyond the door. In short, barely out of the service, we all too often unconsciously declare a moratorium on the fine resolutions that psychic vibrations built for us. And we go along in the usual way until the next Sunday. When that day comes, perhaps we do not even lift the moratorium for the next service; but, instead, sparing ourselves the humiliation of self-castigation, we go to the country club, or fishing, or merely pitch horse-shoes or carry on some other diversion more important than meditation on our sins.

A world is on fire and faith is faltering. Has God failed us, that we must turn to Caesar for salvation? Or have we failed God, and in the materialistic confusion of economic fog are we turning to Caesar to save us from ourselves?

Perplexed by such thoughts one night in Pittsburgh, while attending an economic conference for church people, I heard a young man from Alabama ask a high dignitary in one of the denominations, "But, don't you think that our real problem is to improve people through religion and the work of the church, rather than to look to government and social controls to make people behave as they should?"

Nor do I forget the reply that came from the dignitary as he responded, "Ah, my boy, you forget that you are dealing with sin. The church and religion have their place, to be sure, but we must be practical about these things." Perhaps that man did not realize that, with his answer, he had moved from the spiritual to the secular in his quest for God.

I once made what I was told was a splendid speech. I did not know it. I was just trying honestly to explain why I thought private enterprise was compatible with Christianity. At the close of the meeting, among the line of those who came up to speak to me were a Priest, a Rabbi, a Lutheran Minister and a Christian Scientist. Each of them, in his own way, thanked me and let me know that I was consistent with the true faith.

But, another man, having read a copy of that speech, some weeks later, wrote me in sorrow, for I was not yet saved. An interchange of letters failed to impress me or to budge him. In his eyes I am damned, no matter what the extent of my works, or how earnest my faith, for I have not followed the formula that alone can save the damned.

Still another, also having read the speech which received wide approval from clergy and laymen both, wrote caustically that I was an "egotistical jackass" who had failed to learn that "service and profit can never go together."

These are only a very few among many experiences that have led me to suspect that there is something seriously wrong. I wonder if it is that man has made himself the pattern and creates God in his own image, imputing to God the human characteristics he thinks God ought to have.

Has man become so immersed in trivialities of religion that he has forgotten or let go of the great, basic fundamentals which alone can provide the common denominator for men of all creeds and faiths? Has our headlong haste for social salvation trapped us into worshipping the creature instead of the Creator?

And then I wonder if, perhaps, God Himself ought not to be permitted to have something to say about Who, What and Where He is. Perhaps you and I should concede, to ourselves, to each other, that no one of us has any monopoly on the wisdom, discernment or insight to know Who, What and Where is God.

In addition to the conflicting testimony on details of the nature and processes of God, is the no less terrifying confusion that arises out of the misunderstanding of facts underlying situations which we seek to correct.

As example of what I mean let me name the report of the World Council of Churches issued in September of 1948.

They met in Amsterdam, Holland; protestants from many parts of the world, human beings with somewhat different ideas of God and the manner in which He should be served and worshipped. Here were human beings freighted with convictions of what is wrong with the world and what should be done to correct it, based on a wide variation in understanding of fact all the way from sheer fantasy to something approaching reality.

Earnest men and women, they worked for days, knelt in prayer, gathered new inspiration and went back to work again. Out of their deliberations came, among others, a report on the "Church and the Disorder of Society." This is one of seven reports which, to quote the composite report, "are the product of long and honest thinking on the part of many Christians from many confessions and from many parts of the world." It has been said that this particular section of the report, on the church and the disorder of society, was prepared largely by a clergyman from England, himself under the spell of socialist-labor domination in that country.

At any rate, a careful study of the report shows clearly that even "long and honest thinking" can lead to terribly mistaken conclusions if there be inadequate understanding of economic facts on which to do the thinking.

This report on the "Church and the Disorder of Society" was hailed with acclaim by many so-called liberal church leaders, who took the report as authentic in its findings and dependable as a basis for social action. The most significant conclusion offered in this part of the report was that the ideologies of both communism and capitalism should be rejected and a middle way found.

The specific indictment of capitalism is that:

1. "Capitalism tends to subordinate what should be the primary task of any economy—the meeting of human needs

—to the economic advantage of those who have the most power over its institutions."

2. "It tends to produce serious inequalities."

3. "It has developed a practical form of materialism in western nations in spite of their Christian background, for it has placed the greatest emphasis upon success in making money."

4. "It has also kept the people of capitalistic countries subject to a kind of fate which has taken the form of such social catastrophies as mass unemployment."

(Page 45: "First Assembly of the World Council of Churches")

To correct these evils it is proposed that we change our economic system, rather than seek for the remedies in spiritual revival. But, the simple truth is that the evils in the four-pointed indictment are neither peculiar to nor inherent in capitalism; and one need not know much of history to be aware of that fact. So long as man's behavior has been recorded, long before capitalism developed, the identical evils existed under all systems. They are found where one finds human beings, more especially so where freedom has developed more rapidly than man's fitness for freedom.

It is as logical and true to charge the above sins to capitalism as it would be to say that divorce is due to Christianity, for it is in Christian America that we have so high a ratio of divorce to marriage. And it would be no more mistaken to say that stealing, murder, rape, arson and the rest are all evils of democracy and that the remedies for these evils are to do away with democracy.

The indictment of capitalism on the ground of failing to produce goods for the meeting of human needs rather than seeking profit for those in control, smacks of the argument for production for use rather than for profit, which has already been answered (p. 44). All production is for use and must be for use. Profit is the incentive used to induce men to produce for use. And, if this charge were true, it would be somewhat difficult to explain why in the very country where the charge is hurled we have the highest and most widely disseminated standard of living in the world.

As for the inequalities, thank God we are not all equal. If nature teaches one truth above others it is that equality means stagnation and death. The incentives that arise out of inequalities are indispensable to human progress and to the benefit of all levels of well-being. The equalities asserted in the Declaration of Independence are not the equalities of endowment, ability, performance and reward of which the report in question wrote.

In the four-fold indictment of capitalism by the World Council, one could substitute the word "freedom" for capitalism and the statements would be as accurate as they are now. One could even use the word "Christianity" in place of capitalism in that indictment and the truth of falsity of the statement would be the same.

The recommendation that we find a middle way between communism and capitalism will be discussed in a later chapter on "The Fallacy of the Middle Way." At this point I simply remind the reader that one "cannot serve two masters." Attempting to reconcile the security, governmental planning and collective property of atheistic communism with freedom, individual initiative and private property under the aegis of Christianity just could not work. The mixed system would move inevitably toward one direction or the other, and it would not be in the direction of freedom, for the very compromise of freedom is the first step toward its betrayal.

It may be that wavering faith in God is responsible in large part for the current emphasis on secular thinking in the church. Or it could be preconceived prejudice or disguised materialism, on the part of leaders who are conventionally high-minded but so enmeshed in altruism as to refuse to be receptive to new revelation.

Whatever the reason may be, thinking secularly to solve spiritual problems is to concede that the power of God is not adequate, that Christianity is an ideal or end beyond our practical reach, and so we must seek a Caesar to do the work of God.

This is not due to bad intentions. There is lack of understanding of economic fact and a tendency to place blame, not where it belongs, but rather where it is most easily placed, and, where, unfortunately, the remedy is not to be found.

It would be far wiser for men to seek remedy for secular ills through the strengthening of faith, than to attempt to compensate for the failures of faith by turning to secular substitutes.

CHAPTER 2

ECONOMIC MISCONCEPTIONS

I SPOKE some years ago to a senior class of the American University in Washington, D. C. One of the students asked me whether I thought it was right for 2% of the people to own 98% of the wealth. I said it would not be right, but was it so? He said, "Of course!" And when I asked him for his authority for the statement, he replied: "Why, that's what everybody is saying."

To make his remark really significant it should be pointed out that this boy was majoring in statistics, a subject which should emphasize factual and accurate sources of information. His instructor sat in the meeting but ventured no support for the boy's wild statement, nor did he make any comment when I tore the statement apart and showed it for the nonsense which it was, and still is.

Much of the confusion and perplexities in our economic situations are due to the fact that people believe so many things that are not true, or, not understanding facts correctly, are easily persuaded to accept distorted versions of the truth.

Among the many economic problems which are made more difficult to solve because of this confusion are the following:

a. *Monopoly:*

This is one of the most abused concepts in economics and the shibboleth of an enormous amount of undeserved and unwise abuse, under cover of which much of the harm done by real monopoly escapes attention. Popular misconceptions direct attention in the wrong directions.

By definition, monopoly is such a degree of control over the supply of a good, commodity or service, as to enable the holder of the control to fix prices, or at least to have considerable influence over prices without regard for competition. It is the ability to control prices through control of supply.

A popular misconception is that monopoly price is necessarily a high price, enabling the seller to gouge the helpless buyer and take exorbitant profits. And there has grown up against monopoly in that sense much the same antagonism that the middle ages held against the lender who took advantage of the destitute borrower, each victim having to take what he could get on whatever terms he was given.

But monopoly price is not necessarily a high price. It is likely to be set at the point where the monopolist makes the greatest profit, net, on his total volume of business. This can easily mean a relatively low price in order to get the large volume of business which will yield the greatest net total profit. Regardless of his control over supply, the monopolist cannot make people buy something which he has priced out of their market. If he wants to sell, he must bring the price within the range of what they are able and willing to pay.

There has been monopoly under capitalism. It is only temporary when in private hands, for the profits supposed to exist attract the competition of other enterprisers whose additional supply of the monopolized or of some other competing product subsequently forces the price down. Under our system such situations can be corrected without government control. If, however, the monopoly is complete, as in the case of a gas company or telephone exchange, without competing service, then regulation by law may become necessary.

The government of the United States passed such laws in 1890 and again in 1912, known as the "anti-trust laws," aimed at conspiracy in restraint of trade. Those laws have been proved affective, sufficiently so that Thurman Arnold, who spent some time enforcing the laws under the Franklin D. Roosevelt regime, said that there were no private monopolies left in the United States outside of the utilities under government regulation.

Another misconception of monopoly is the confusion or the identification of big business as monopoly. Indeed, big business may owe its very size to the fact that it is not a monopoly, but has had to fight so hard for its life that it developed greater efficiency than all of its competitors. The big concern whose management has not developed commensurately with its growth of business may be at a disadvantage in competition with the smaller, flexible and more intimately managed business whose top management can keep in close contact with every situation within the business. Such smaller business can make a large company work very hard for the business it gets. The great United States Steel Company, once regarded as a monopoly, has been able to stay in business because it kept itself competitive through improving management and comparable service.

Size by itself is not monopolistic in the determination of price, although it can mean a larger than average share of the total volume of business in an industry. It is also necessary in some industries to do an efficient job for the consumer if at all. Neither small nor large business can really prosper without each other. And it is throwing dust in our eyes to denounce big business as monopoly per se.

People do not really object to monopoly as such. When the monopoly gives them lower postal rates, or electric light rates, telephone or gas rates, than they could have from competing companies who would have to duplicate expensive service equipment and organization, they insist on monopoly service.

LABOR MONOPOLY

The organized worker in brickwork, carpentry, plastering and the rest, is usually against monopoly as such, but he loves it in the labor union. It is ironic that labor leaders who denounce the monopoly they claim exists in industry bigness, themselves exercise the most complete monopoly in our history, outside of government monopoly itself. In many crafts and industries labor leaders possess a more complete and firm control over the supply of labor than ever an industrialist exercised over raw materials or finished goods.

That is not to argue that we must do away with labor unions. It is to signify that control there can be as effective and as bad as it could in other hands and in other places. Even in labor we should prevent combinations in restraint of trade, or fair competition. Labor as well as management should be subject to anti-trust laws.

MONOPOLY NOT INHERENT IN CAPITALISM

It is apparent that what the opponent of monopoly really opposes is the *kind* of monopoly he does not like or *where* he does not like it or under leadership of which he is suspicious. But he is usually willing to benefit by monopoly even at the expense of others. And that is not the fault or weakness of an economic system. It is part of the price we pay for freedom and the penalty we suffer when freedom is given to people who are not fully ready for it. It is an indication of the great importance of another factor which has to do with human behavior under freedom. In short, the problem is moral and spiritual rather than economic.

MONOPOLY DESTROYS ITSELF

Monopoly in any free society is bound to destroy itself through the inefficiencies that develop out of lack of need for effort to meet competition, or the arousing of greater efforts by competitors, or the attention of government stepping in to regulate monopoly.

GOVERNMENT MONOPOLY

The most effective and costly of monopolies is the government monopoly. There are fiscal justifications offered for government monopoly, such as the salt or tobacco monopolies of some countries, which in effect are means of taxing the people through the higher prices charged for commodities controlled by the government. As a rule, government monopoly is like any other government enterprise, relatively inefficient and costly to the public. Were it not for the coercion of force behind government, this type of monopoly would go the way of private monopoly where trade is free of coercive restraints.

b. *Who Pays for What:*

One of the greatest injuries ever done to the American people was to teach them that the way to prosperity is to do less work in fewer hours, that through government control of prices and projects we could have more by producing less, and have it at the expense of those who already have too much. The formula varies, but in any form it carries the idea that government control enables the worker to get something for nothing.

Limitation of output comes finally out of the worker's own pocket, for his purchasing power consists of what he produces; and all he can buy with his purchasing power is that which is produced by other workers. In a complex economy like ours it may take a long time, or what seems a long time, for the effect to work its way back to the cause, but it finally does just that. We can use no more than is produced, and if we produce less we have less to consume. There is no magic in government to controvert that fact.

What seems like proof that we are better off through government control and limitation of production, is only the consequence of living for a while on accumulated wealth, as the person who diets can live for a while on accumulated fat. And while this is being done, it is usually accompanied by inflation and rise of government debt and government control, which finally exact an extra penalty for the very delay in arriving at the day of settlement.

An unhappy fallacy that plays into the hands of the collectivists is the belief that the rich individuals and corporations can be taxed to relieve the workers of taxes they would otherwise have to pay. Politicians are mortally afraid of the sales tax because it plays no favorites, but hits everybody, and is especially disagreeable to people who would otherwise not be conscious of the taxes they pay. So the manipulators of public feeling have played on the theme of "soak the rich." Books have been written and articles circulated to prove that the few top incomes get nearly all the income and the mass of people get only the remaining crumbs. Politicians have played this theme to get themselves elected. They promise to tax the corporations and to levy no burden on the poor.

But the policies which result from efforts to load the top and relieve the bottom in the scale of incomes, even beyond proportionate payments in relation to income, are likely ultimately to destroy both the top and the bottom.

It is true that those at the top receive more per person than do those at the bottom. It has always been so where freedom has given men opportunity to exercise their differences in ability and industry. And so it always will be so long as freedom lives and so long as men are not alike.

A progressive tax, with the rate of tax per dollar of income rising as the income rises, so that those with higher incomes not only pay taxes on more dollars of income but also pay more taxes on every dollar of income that is taxed, has something to be said for it. It is true that the bare necessities of life constitute a higher proportion of the low incomes and a relatively lower proportion of the high incomes. The rich, or what is left of them, can afford to pay somewhat more in taxes than can the poor.

But there is a limit, which many economists believe has already been reached. Taxes for the higher incomes are now confiscatory, and even those on middle bracket incomes are so high that incentive to earn more has disappeared in many cases. That means a decline in savings and investment, and subsequent decline in tools, jobs and earning opportunities for the great mass of workers.

With the corporations the picture is worse. Radical leaders shout that we must take all the taxes we need from the corporations. But they overlook or ignore the fact that the taxes taken from corporations have to come out of prices of the products. In the last analysis it is John Q. Public, the customer or buyer, who pays the corporation taxes in the prices of the goods he buys. These taxes may never be seen, yet their burden can be crushing, for they are wrapped up in the so-called "hidden taxes" which constitute an ever-rising portion of the prices paid for goods bought by the workers. At the present writing those taxes amount to about $800 per year per family. And that is only part of the burden which every worker has to bear.

When the government taxes away earnings and profits that should go back into industry to create more tools and more and better jobs, it is really eating our seed corn. It is thereby preventing the larger crop of prosperity we could have if those seeds of profits and investments were planted in industry instead of used up by government.

Where shall additional taxes come from?

Figures developed in 1951 indicate that increase of taxes will have to come largely from those persons whose incomes are less than $5,000 a year. In fact, about 86% of the additional taxes on income will have to come from that group, while only about 14% of the potential increase can come from those persons whose incomes are above $5,000 a year. That is because the federal government has already run the well nearly dry in the upper brackets and additional income must therefore be taken largely from the enormous pool made up of the many incomes under $5,000 a year.

It is stupid to expect many fish from a pool where there are only a few fish. Wise fishermen drop their lines where the fish are plentiful, and a government, facing the need for more income, had better seek that income where it is to be found.

Of course politicians shrink from taxing directly the groups who have the most votes. The remaining alternative is for government TO SPEND LESS. And if people with incomes under $5,000 a year knew the truth, that the benefit they get from government spending costs more than it is worth, and that additional money for more benefits must come from the mass of people themselves, they would clamor for reduction in government spending. They might even refuse to be deceived into believing the cry of heavier taxes for the rich, lower taxes for the poor, and greater benefits for those who cannot pay for them at all.

All taxes come finally out of production. That is one reason why the power to tax is the power to destroy.

A great fallacy is the belief that government, by some magic, can provide charity or individual welfare at lower cost than can the people themselves. This fallacy is based on the assumption that government produces more from less. The truth is that the government is inefficient, with a very high cost of operation per unit of satisfaction rendered. For every dollar of benefit given in subsidies, more than two dollars ultimately has to be collected from the taxpayer. It does not seem to make good sense for anyone to spend fifty-two cents out of his dollar in order to get back forty-eight cents or less as an apparent gift. But that is what government grants and subsidies mean. The unhappy truth is that the government takes away more and gives back less than would be the case if people handled their own giving to those in need.

c. *Inflation:*

Inflation is the great bugaboo. For years we have been warning each other of the terrible dangers of inflation. And inflation has gone right on, debauching our currency, raising prices, destroying savings and wiping out the protection of insurance policies, while raising government debt for future generations to pay.

Inflation will never be stopped or even mitigated until it is rightly understood.

Because its effects in raising prices are so easily seen, inflation is often misrepresented as consisting of higher prices. The effect is mistaken for the cause, and when government tries to cure inflation by arbitrarily holding prices to a level, the remedy is wrong. The effort is like that of the witch doctor who tries to purify the blood by cutting off the pimples it produces.

High prices are the result* of inflation, not the cause. Inflation itself is the "puffing up" or "blowing up" of the supply of money available for the purchase of goods. Thus, if the government prints money or raises money by borrowing through the issue of government bonds, and uses the money to pay the costs of government,

---

*High prices result from a number of causes, among which inflation is one of the most important and probably the most dangerous. Other causes are scarcity of goods, increasing demand for goods, rising costs of production,

salaries, materials and all the rest, the medium of exchange is inflated, or puffed up, by the amount of money so created and used.

It is also inflation if that money is used to buy arms and ammunition and pay soldiers, to carry on a war. But it is not inflation if the government raises the money by taxation, for then the total medium of exchange remains the same in amount, and the money used to pay the expenses of government simply has been collected from money already in existence and in the possession of the citizens who give it up in taxes.

If people raise the prices of stocks by speculatively bidding up those prices in the stock market, and buy the higher-priced stocks by discounting notes (borrowing) at the banks, the result is to inflate the medium of exchange. (See Chapter 3 of Part II: How Bankers Create Money.) That was what happened during the great inflation of the nineteen-twenties, when billions of dollars of credit money were created by discounting notes against the rising value of stocks and bonds.

But if a manufacturer borrows money from a bank, also by discounting his note, to finance the production of more goods which will be available for purchase by those in whose hands the new money falls, and later pays back the loan with money received from the sale of the goods so produced, it is not inflation. That is expansion and contraction of the medium of exchange, adjusting itself to already existing needs of commerce and trade. There is no dilution of the purchasing power of money.

Dilution is the test of inflation. When the government pours additional money into circulation the result is to dilute the purchasing power of every dollar already in existence. It is like pouring water into a can of milk. It still looks like milk, but we have to drink more glasses of it to get as many calories as were in the glass before it was diluted.

That is why inflation is such a terrible economic disease. It is a kind of anemia, or loss of life-giving corpuscles. Colleges, churches and other institutions relying on fixed income from investments are the victims of legalized theft as inflation reduces the purchasing power of their income, just as surely as is the widow whose bread is snatched from her table by the dilution of purchasing power on which her living depends.

Inflation takes away from consumers generally the benefits of lower prices that would otherwise result from increased productivity and greater volume of goods produced. No less serious is the deceptive misinterpretation which the inflaters place on the stabilizing of prices, when increased production conceals the effects of inflation. For inflation would have raised the prices if increased production had not held those prices down in spite of the lowered purchasing power of the dollar.

The inflaters take to themselves the credit which really belongs to industry for holding prices down, and then they blame industry for the inflation for which they are themselves responsible, if industry is unable to increase production efficiency and volume of output enough to absorb and so conceal the effects of inflation.

So, in many directions, inflation demoralizes the entire economic structure and ultimately destroys even the moral undergirding of that structure.

Price control is futile as a cure for inflation. What price control really does is to force the sale of something at a price below what is needed to meet rising costs. The result is to discourage production, and so the supply is reduced. Since the price is held down while more and more money goes into circulation, demand for the articles produced is bound to go up. And then we have the double upward pressure on prices resulting from diminishing supply and increasing demand. Prices are bound to go up, or goods will go into the black markets to satisfy demand at prices higher than those fixed by the government.

It makes popular political appeal to say that we shall not permit anyone to charge more for the goods we buy, or rent for the places we occupy, but it has no real effect in holding inflation. There is no satisfaction in low prices for steaks if there are no steaks for the consumer to buy.

Trying to stop inflation by holding down prices, while pouring more money into circulation, is like trying to hold down the steam pressure in a tea kettle by sitting on the lid while turning up the fire underneath. There will be interesting results, but the steam pressure will not be held down. It will increase until the lid goes up and the sitter with it.

The way to stop the steam pressure in that tea kettle is to turn off the fire under the kettle. By the same token, the way to stop inflation is to stop the flooding of our medium of exchange with more and more money.

The most important single factor causing inflation during the past 20 years has been government spending. When business borrows money it does so to produce more goods and there are additional goods available for the new money that the borrowing brings into existence. Then when the newly produced goods are sold, the borrowed credit is paid back to the bank and the new money goes out of existence. That is expansion and contraction. Production brings new goods into existence with the new money from expansion, and the goods go out of existence as they are consumed, and the money contracts.

But when government borrows money it spends the millions into circulation by buying goods and services. The goods and services are used up, but the new money stays in circulation. That is inflation.

A reduction of the federal budget, elimination of needless enormous waste in government spending, could do more to stop inflation than all the price controls put together. The use of wage controls together with price controls could help, because of the effect on costs, but are even more difficult to administer and much less welcome to the worker.

If given the right of way, the Federal Reserve Board, with its power to influence credits, could help materially to stop inflation. But that could not happen so long as the Treasury Department were using the Federal Reserve System to hold up the prices of government bonds by purchase of bonds in the open market. Every time the Treasury Department so buys a bond more new money goes into circulation and further dilutes the purchasing power of money already in circulation. This is so because the bond purchased is discounted with the Federal Reserve Bank and the new money issued against the bond is used to pay for it.

Tremendous suffering and hardship could be avoided, or at least mitigated, if those who have to deal with inflation at its source recognized the true causes, and dealt with those causes as an economic problem—rather than use inflation as a short-cut to economic recovery, or to establish political controls.

It is important to realize that the inflation of the two past decades

(1930's and 1940's), which has already diluted the purchasing power of our money to less than one-half of what it was, was neither necessary nor unavoidable. It was the result of a policy deliberately chosen by a political administration to raise money for its reckless spending, apparently without regard for the consequences, and after a solemn promise to reduce government spending.

The frightful danger in controls is that they are difficult to remove, and themselves constitute a sure way to socialism. The more controls we have, and the longer we have them, the more difficult it becomes to get along without them, and the less likelihood there is of restoring freedom.

The surest way to stop socialism is to reduce the amount of money for the socialists to spend. It takes a great deal of money to carry on the debilitating and enervating paternalisms on which socialism depends, and the most effective way to stop the process is to cut off the flow of money which finances it.

d. The National Debt:

The danger in debt is more than its immensity. It is the complacency of people in contemplating that debt. It is bad enough that the federal debt already amounts to more than 260 billion dollars, or about $7,000 per family for our entire population; an amount which will take more than a hundred years to pay, if it is paid at all. What has made it worse is the changed attitude toward debt. People were encouraged to forget that the debt would have to be paid out of production which is our standard of living and to forget even that it had to be paid at all. There was fostered the stupid idea that debt, instead of being a liability is an asset or basis of prosperity. Economists as well as bureaucrats have advocated increase in government debt and monetization of that debt whenever we need more money in circulation, instead of relying on bank loans and other private sources of funds.

To illustrate: suppose you and I owed each other $2,000. Being sensible people, we could simply cancel each other's debt and call it square. But that is not the ultra-modern way which looks on government debt as a working asset. Instead of paying each other off by cancellation of both debts, we would encourage the making of debt. Thus, since you owe me $2,000, I am worth $2,000. Since I owe you $2,000, you are worth $2,000. The total wealth is $4,000. Now,

let's have each of us owe the other $10,000, and the total wealth
is $20,000. Then we might take our notes to the federal reserve bank,
and if we had the proper influence and could persuade the bank that
our notes were good commercial paper, we might discount the notes
and get almost another $20,000, making the total wealth about
$40,000. Isn't it wonderful?

Silly as that seems, it is the kind of reasoning that lay back of
considering our federal debt an asset and an assurance of security
and prosperity for the United States, as was stated by an Assistant
Secretary of the U. S. Treasury in Chicago in March of 1950.

Nevertheless, debts are still debts, liabilities that honest people
pay. And when a government falls short of the degree of honor that
impels an individual to pay his debts, we lay the ground work for
further lack of morals and integrity in high places, in and out of
government.

e. *Depression:*

THE PROBLEM

One of the most serious problems in any economic society is depression, the decline in employment and production that finally brings
an entire economy to a stuttering halt. Much attention has been given
to this problem, with far from satisfactory result.

Here, as with inflation, it is a serious mistake to try to cure the
ill by dealing with symptoms instead of causes. Merely dividing the
work, or reducing hours while raising rates of pay, taxing the not
yet destitute to support the destitute while the destitute become less
concerned about doing what is needed to correct their condition,
guaranteed annual pay with no provision for making the pay possible, and all the other measures used to alleviate the results of the
depression, are finally of little or no avail. More often than not they
simply aggravate the problem for the future.

The answer to depression must be sought in the business cycle,
but it is not of the business cycle. If we take for granted that
nothing can be done about the business cycle we might as well drop
our efforts to remedy the situation.

On the other hand, I doubt that we can do away with the business
cycle. I doubt that we can do away entirely with depression; but we
can take measures to mitigate greatly through increasing knowledge
and understanding and the strengthening of self-control. We can

prevent much of the unemployment of tomorrow by foregoing the excesses of today.

There are four periods in the business cycle: the period of recovery, the period of prosperity, the period of crisis and recession, and the period of depression. Each grows out of the previous period and sets in motion factors and forces which bring about the succeeding period, in the order named, over and over again.

An important fact to keep in mind in dealing with the business cycle and any problems that arise out of it, is that all business is done on the principle of anticipation. If all goods were made only as purchased, or all goods made were purchased, we could escape depression. But, in order to have the benefits of mass production, we must produce in anticipation of purchases, we must estimate as accurately as we can how much we should produce or how much stock we should carry. Also, at once we involve highly specialized industries, the extensive use of credit, a complex interdependence of all business and industry, all of which, combined with freedom of choice by the consumer, bring about a degree of uncertainty which makes depression possible. Dealing with each and all of these related factors, steps can be taken to mitigate depression in some measure, but none of them really strikes at the root of the difficulty.

If we work backward from the depression itself, to preceding and apparently casual situations, we can see what needs to be modified in order to correct the situation.

Following the period of recovery, during which liquidation of assets has been completed, and new forces set in motion to encourage economic activity, comes the period of prosperity. Now production and employment are high, profits are distributed, savings accumulate, investments increase with expanding volume of business, and everything seems to be functioning smoothly. Then, suddenly, a crisis develops; people slow up on buying, business declines, here and there a concern reduces its operations or closes its doors because it is unable to repay a loan; the people who are discharged buy less and cause further failures, and soon we find ourselves sliding down into a depression. The overt act that usually begins the entire process is slowing down of buying by consumers.

The key to depression is enforced liquidation of debts. If buying could pick up before notes had to be met, the enforced liquidation might be avoided, and if the enforced liquidation could be prevented there would be no sudden or considerable unemployment and decline of business activity due to necessary curtailments. So we seek for the cause of enforced liquidations.

REMEDY THROUGH BALANCE OF FREE EXCHANGE

Enforced liquidations appear when business concerns, having enlarged their activities on credit, which has to be repaid, discover that the income due to sales is not sufficient to enable them to pay their bills. They are likely to have large quantities of goods on hand which they have not been able to sell at regular prices. But the goods on hand cannot be used to pay bills. They must first be sold to raise the money for paying bills and debts. And this has to be done in a market which has already fallen away so much that they were not able to sell their goods at regular prices. The answer is to sell them at a loss. So the goods are sacrificed, and then production is curtailed because there is a dearth of funds with which to continue operations. This throws more men out of work. Then the enforced liquidation in these concerns is followed by enforced liquidation in others who suffer because they in turn lose business and in turn throw more men out of work.

If all the goods made had been sold in regular and orderly manner, there would have been no need to sacrifice inventories at less than cost prices in order to raise funds to pay bills and debts. What is missing in BALANCE in the economic order. If all the goods produced by all the businesses had been exchanged for each other, and that is the way they must finally be sold, there would have been no need for liquidation. So we must seek a way to balance the economic order for complete exchange of goods. Then there will be no more depression.

But how shall our economy be balanced? In a totalitarian state, someone can sit down and diagram what each concern is to manufacture, what quantities of raw materials and labor it must have, machinery and tools and the rest, and even assign the output among prospective buyers, making each take the allotted quantity.

That would be regimented production and distribution. But we could not stop there. We must also regiment the consumer, telling him what he must use and how much of each item. Then the totalitarian can dispose of all the product, determined by him in the first place, and there would be no more depression. But freedom would also disappear, and the people regimented would in effect become slaves and have to accept the lowered standards of living that would inexorably follow the regimentation. That is what government control would mean.

On the other hand, while freedom induces maximum production and activity, the very fact of freedom, or the right to choose for one's self, makes it difficult to bring about the balance we need to make and exchange just the right quality of everything. That is why we shall not do away entirely with depression in a free country, or any country of free men, so long as we insist on the benefits of mass production. For mass production necessitates reliance on the principle of anticipation and that brings in its wake all the uncertainties which make a depression possible.

But, we can very much mitigate the depression and escape the major portion of its ill effects, without doing away with our freedom to choose. There is not room here for a detailed explanation of method, but it would mean supplying every individual concern within each industry, through its trade association or other agency, with reports on the basis of which reasonably accurate anticipation of demand could be calculated, and production adjusted from time to time to shifting changes from earlier anticipations. Once the information was made available, we would have to rely on the profit motive to induce business men to follow sensible courses of action, entirely on their own volition. This would not be easy, for there are rigidities of mind and emotion which would delay and make more difficult the acceptance of even indisputably sound courses of action.

The effect of these rigidities in our economic structure would be to resist and even prevent adjustments necessary to maintain among the different groups of producers the reciprocal relationships which, in turn, would facilitate the total exchange of all goods produced. For the most part, these reciprocal relationships are revealed and can be measured in terms of cost to produce and the prices resulting from those costs.

Thus, a group which enjoys special privileges, usually in consequence of concessions from government, may for a time collect tribute from other groups. After a time, however, such a group is likely to price itself out of the market and set in motion the beginnings of a depression by the accumulation of inventory or by actually throwing men out of work.

The accumulation of certain unsold or more slowly selling goods in the market may result from raising costs due to non-recriprocally higher wages in the group producing those goods. It may also result from changing tastes and desires among consumers, or from the appearance of newly competing goods more efficiently produced or more attractive to the consumers.

In any case, such accumulation are a warning signal that prices should be lowered, or products changed or even withdrawn from the market. To meet such a situation requires a flexible wage scale as well as managerial adaptability.

The economy must be sufficiently flexible to respond to indications of depression before the disease passes out of control. And that flexibility can be attained only in a free market, uninhibited by government control and with people willing to relax their individual rigidities of interest in behalf of the common good. Wages and salaries, as well as prices and production, must be flexible whenever flexibility is needed to prevent or at least mitigate otherwise disastrous depression.

As these rigidities were overcome, through a process of education and experience, business men could adjust their schedules of production, costs and prices, borrowing, buying and selling, inventories and related policies, to anticipate the changed demands. Some of them would cheat, but competition could go on and freedom not be curtailed, because the enforcing power would be self-control and self-determination. In a sentence, the advantage would be that we would make the necessary adjustments more frequently and with less distortion in exchange and inventories, or lack of balance, and so avoid the terrible liquidations that have developed in the past. In previous depressions we have delayed so long and consequently developed such high tension in our economy as to make the necessary adjustments of production and sales impossible except by throwing millions of men out of work. We would now substitute a series of potential and incipient depressions, each of relatively little consequence, in place of the catastrophic recessions that have marked our previous depressions.

The difference can be illustrated by a clock. The present situation, with uncontrolled depressions, is like a clock with a very long pendulum and a wide arc through which that pendulum sweeps from one extreme to the other, with terrible and momentous changes each way. *Yet, the pendulum must swing if the clock is to go.* Likewise there must be changes and adjustments if we are not to fall into a static and dying economy.

But, suppose the pendulum were shorter and the arc through which it swings were narrow, with very little difference in position between extremes. The clock would still go, just as the economy would still function. But the adjustments would come so frequently and be so moderate that the pendulum, and the economy, would be hovering closely on either side of a norm. The smaller and more frequent adjustments would avoid most of the suffering and loss that follow in the wake of extreme variations with their terrible tensions.

There is still much to learn of the business cycle, but we are learning. It is significant that the real answer to depression, as in many other economic problems, is not a mere change in mechanics of the system, but rather in the behavior of people who live within the system.

We do not need to build up intricate and intimate government controls. Indeed, such controls defeat their avowed purpose. We do need improved individuals, with better and wide-spread understanding, higher moral standards and more effective self-control. Partial or mistaken remedies, such as governmental tampering with economic processes to win votes and remain in power, simply postpone the inevitable. While the remedy suggested here, in principle, seems long and difficult, it is the ultimate answer; and the sooner we begin to seek it and apply it, the sooner we shall remedy the age-old ills. Had the disciples and followers of Jesus, down through the ages, actually lived and thus demonstrated the validity of His teachings, they would long ago have solved problems that government controls only muddy with worse ills.

PART FOUR—TRIUMPH OF FAITH IN FACT

Chapter 1

ACCORDING TO YOUR FAITH

a. *Faith the Root of Human Action:*

Man's actions grow out of his faith. Merely to live requires faith. One could not eat or drink, rest or walk, think or talk, or make choices in any direction, except on faith. We must believe something or we die. Through faith we can take unto ourselves the attributes of greatness. We live by what we believe so long as we are satisfied with the results or so long as it works. When what we believe no longer works we change to some other belief in the hope that the new tenet is right and will work better.

So we make our choices on the basis of our faith. And we do choose. Even when we are denied alternatives in action, as under the dictates of a tyrant, we can still choose whether or not to obey. But the choices with which we build character are those which we make voluntarily among the several alternatives before us. Character, as it is built up, becomes a pattern for conduct; it is a crystallization of faith expressed in a myriad of choices in many directions, which almost automatically makes further choices by habit. Therein lies the enormous importance of individual character as the backbone of national life.

The choices we make and the actions we take, determine our relationships with other human beings, with the world in which we live and even with God. This is true even though we cannot see or foretell the consequences of our choices or those consequences prove very different from what we had hoped or planned. The law of cause and effect, as fundamental and irrevocable as the law of gravity, does not take into account any motives, hopes, desires or intentions. For every cause, be it thought, feeling or act, the law follows through with the appropriate result.

Hence, since it is the genesis of choice, faith is the root of human action and its consequences.

Jesus saw this very clearly and, with His utter integrity in going right to the root of every matter with which he dealt, he sought to imbue men with the faith they needed to effect the purpose of God in man.

175

Whether you accept the divinity of Jesus in consequence of His immaculate conception and birth by a virgin, or because you believe that He achieved divinity through spiritual growth in communion with God while housed within a human body which had to be disciplined and mastered to His purpose, or a combination of them, you must accord Him the factual attributes of divinity. Believing that He was sent to rescue the world, you must no less believe that His vision and understanding are both of devine origin; and that neither could be limited to the brief period during which He lived and moved among men in the flesh. He saw far beyond those years. In order merely to inaugurate, even though He could not then accomplish His mission in full, He must have understood what was necessary to redeem man and how ultimately to bring about that redemption.

It is tremendously significant, then, that Jesus concerned Himself with individual human beings and not with mass movements or with political or economic organizations. He dealt with the individual human being in his relation with God and other individuals. He revealed the individual as free to make his own choices and decisions, responsible to God for the consequences of those choices and decisions. This was high testimony that the movements which sweep the world, the organizations and institutions which pattern the economic, social and political life of man, are all the fruit of individual choices born of the faiths by which men live. From which it follows that the redemption of the world, the overcoming of evil and its effects, is to be accomplished through the character and conduct of the individual human being in the aggregate.

Jesus showed that man may live in the world and yet not be of the world, in that he can overcome the world with the triumph of spirit through faith. This indicates clearly that the precepts of religion must come from God as He reveals His will in the nature of things as they are, or in whatever other way He may see fit. Those precepts must not be subordinated to mere worldly purposes, but rather guide the individual in his utilization of even worldly things in serving his stewardship to God.

The path to redemption lies not through government by men or social control which relieves the individual of responsibility for his own welfare and redemption, but rather through the voluntary acceptance of stewardship by the individual and the self-initiated and self-directed development of character in obedience to God. Following the example of Jesus, we would not try to improve man through government planning and social control, but would seek to have better government and to lift the level of national life through the voluntary improvement of character and self-realization of the individual human being as a member of society.

b. *The Common Denominator:*

Man cannot live unto himself, alone. While it is true that society is made up of individuals and the total is a composite of the sum of the nature of those individuals, and any efforts to correct abuses or raise the standards of existence must deal with individuals as such, improving society through the voluntary betterment and development of individual character, it is no less true that the very nature of man demands that he live as a member of society.

The history of man's development and progress from savagery demonstrates the tremendous importance of cooperation among individuals, the need for something to hold men knit in groups even while they function as individuals.

It is as man has developed and submitted himself to law and order, as he built the arts and cultivated the sciences of civilization, that he has pushed back the edges of the jungle from which he emerged.

But the jungle is always there, ready to crowd back over the areas that civilization has won from it. The savage in man is subdued and held under cover by a precariously thin veneer of principle fashioned into habit and tradition. He is not yet completely cooperative and is not fully ready for the terrible responsibilities of freedom. The energies of men, like the wild-running power of a cataract, need to be harnessed lest they destroy the civilization men have built. Unless self-mastery goes hand in hand with the release of spirit and volition, the very freedom which results becomes destructive.

There is a wide variation in the degree of individual self-control. So there must be coordination. Just as gravity holds a physical world together, men of vision and understanding must supply the elements of coherence to hold individuals together in a frame-work of order and justice. The element of coherence may be some commonly accepted principle, a common interest, fear, purpose or idea. Historically, at one time or another, each of these has so served, and always, whichever it may be, it has arisen out of man's sense of inadequacy, his feeling that his own strength is not enough and he knows not where to turn to fortify himself. He welcomes the positive declaration of authority that relieves him of the necessity of solving the problem and suffering the consequences of failure to solve it. Authority must be exercised through human beings, whether it be through power of some men over others or voluntary acceptance by those who recognize the authority.

Leadership springs up in many ways, but is usually the response to an actual need. The leader may be discovered by those whose void for authority recognizes the leader as sufficiently expert or possessed of prestige or other qualifications which endow him with the sanction necessary for authority. Sometimes the leader, exploiting his knowledge of the people, can arouse the emotions and instincts that will in turn demand him as leader. Or he may use the force of fear or hope to win acceptance for an idea to which he is committed. In any case, however, leadership usually moves into rather than springs out of government. For leadership implies voluntary acceptance of the leader by those whom he leads.

Government is more likely to grow out of leadership. Seeking to perpetuate the power which his leadership presently gives him, the leader may set up or gain control of government and then rely on the force of government to secure continued acceptance of and obedience to himself through that government. The result is what we call "government by men." The power in that government, wielded by an individual who has graduated from leadership, is likely to corrupt the individual who exercises it. He begins to mistake his desires for natural law, his own ideas of what is right or wrong, or is best for the people, for the wisdom of a superior being. Though high motives may impel his actions, he still makes himself a ruler and even a despot.

That kind of power, or the force in government that gives it strength, is effective in direct ratio to its interference with individual freedom. What was originally leadership becomes domination by the individual through the force of government, and the trend of individual development of those governed is reversed. Individual liberty and responsibility recede.

The one advantage of such government is that it DOES provide law and order, without which the individual cannot develop nearly so well. But at best, it is, or should be, a stage of transition, holding society together under forms of law while we endeavor to establish the proper basis for order and justice.

The most effective efforts of human beings come from voluntary initiative, motivated by some instinct or desire within the individual. This is much more powerful than even the force of government, since the unanimity and cooperation of which human beings are capable, once aroused will sweep the strongest government before it. The greater power lies in the fact that the unanimity and cooperation are spontaneous and require only to be touched off. After that they act automatically. On the other hand, the force of government has to give notice of itself. At best it works indirectly on the motives and instincts within the individual, by use of force in denying or suppressing the voluntary expressions of instinct, possibly through fear of punishment, or even death. That process activates emotions, such as hate or fear of punishment and so discourages uprisings by cowing those who might rebel.

The voluntary unanimity and cooperation of individuals therefore is the most effective element in holding masses together. But it is difficult to secure that unanimity and cooperation. Here again, we find ourselves going back to the faith by which we live. And so long as desires, hopes and aims grow out of conflicting faiths, it will remain difficult to bring and hold masses of men together. The use of government to maintain order and justice, therefore, contributes to our transition from habits of the jungle to the ultimate liberty confirmed in self-control. It is a worth while transition.

What we need to find while we hold men together as best we can, and discourage the outlets of greed and war as fully as possible, is a COMMON DENOMINATOR of faith and hope.

It has been said that it does not matter what the common denominator is, just so long as we find it. But, that is not true. For a common denominator can be that only if it reaches more deeply into the well-springs of life for the individual than any of the other elements that compete for the interest of man.

Since man's choices grow out of his faith, and in turn build character, with the combination of desires, instincts, habits and principles, a common religious faith would provide the perfect common denominator for all men.

Nor are we so far from the possibility of realizing such a common denominator. We do not need to reconcile all the variations among denominations and faiths. We need only to begin with the commandment basic to them all. The rest will follow, for, as the Master assured us, he who would know the doctrine has only to do the will of the Father. And doing the will of the Father begins with accepting the Father as our God beside Whom we will have no other gods.

The First Commandment is the great common denominator.

CHAPTER 2

CONTRIBUTION OF CHRISTIANITY
TO
PRIVATE COMPETITIVE ENTERPRISE

OUT of the long evolution of increasing utilization of human time and energy in making things more useful for the satisfaction of human wants, came a system called "Capitalism." In the United States this economic system is more accurately described as "Private Competitive Enterprise," since "Capitalism" is the word that should be used to designate the productive process within the economic system.

Under that system we have prospered as no other people on earth have ever prospered. With less than 7% of the world's population, we Americans have almost 50% of the total production of the world. No less important, we have raised the share of the total industrial production going to workers from less than 40% in 1850 to more than 80% in 1929 and possibly 85% in 1953. Our people are better off than any other people in the world; for an hour of work in America buys more goods than can an hour of work anywhere else on earth.

However, the same factors and forces that made possible our unparalleled prosperity also brought in their train less pleasant consequences. Depressions with unemployment, and even destitution in the midst of apparent prosperity, have marred our record.

There are those who deplore the differences in individual income and consequent position in life, a difference which provides incentive to greater production, and which many of us welcome as contributing to improvement in all levels of living. By the same critics, crime, suffering, injustice and all manner of evil existing in our country are often charged as inescapable consequences of the economic system we have mistakenly called "capitalism."

Many earnest and eloquent, even though inadequately informed, leaders would correct or remove these evils by having us discard our economic system. They would substitute in its place some other system from the waste-basket of history, as the cure-all to bring

181

the "blessings of equality and social justice" in place of the evils
we now endure.

As part of the movement for some form of collective control
over our economic life, radical agitators working with and through
well-intentioned reformers, have succeeded in attaching discredit
to our economic system by building horrible pictures of a thing
they called "capitalism." The very word has been given a bad odor
and so used to damn the economic system to which the very masses
before whom it has been pilloried owe the highest standard of
living that workers have yet known. The despoilers of the word
"capitalism" have done what is comparable to giving a good dog a
bad name. Ignoring its excellent qualities, they have smeared it with
lies and kicked it into disrepute.

It may now be impossible to undo entirely the wrong that has
been done to straight thinking by the way in which exploiters of
public opinion have spewed their rancor on a word. But, before our
religious and social reformers inaugurate any program for the renewal of society through modification or destruction of our economic
system, they should fully and accurately inform themselves on the
nature of American private competitive enterprise and what makes
it function as it does.

In the interests of truth and accuracy let me point out that what
is conveniently thought of as "capitalism" in America, is much
more and far more complex than merely "capitalism." It is a way of
life in which there are elements that make it different from the so-
called capitalism of other countries. Those elements are not inherently
part of capitalism at all, but arise from sources that constitute essential characteristics in our American Way of Life. They exist side by
side with the process of production that is properly called "Capitalism." The economic system in which capitalism is part should properly
be spoken of as "Private Competitive Enterprise."

Capitalism, pure and simple, is the use of the products of past
industry for the further production of goods. It involves, first, the
production of a profit, or a surplus over the cost of production. Production must add to the materials used a greater utility than that
which is consumed in the process of production.

Second, out of that surplus, or profit, we must lay aside a portion which we call savings. And third, out of the savings we either

make or buy tools and machinery, or we buy additional materials or hire more labor, or a combination of part or all of them. In one way or another the savings drawn out of profit are used to make more goods with a given amount of human time and energy. That is the process that should rightly be called "capitalism."

What we call "capital" consists of the goods already produced or the money for which they were sold. They are the products of past industry, of labor which is already paid for, and are used in producing more goods.

The "capitalist" is the person who owns capital goods, whether or not he uses them himself. His ownership of them makes him the capitalist. Whether or not he knows or is willing to admit it, the carpenter who owns his tools, the little store-keeper or anyone with savings in the bank or owning any bonds or shares of stock in an enterprise, be it ever so little, is just as truly a capitalist as the head of a great manufacturing concern. The difference is in degree, not in kind.

There we have the essentials. Any features beyond those described in the preceding four paragraphs are not inherent in or necessary to capitalism; even though they make one economic system different from others by their presence or absence. The distinguishing features in our system are due to religious, ethical and social backgrounds out of which we take the principles by which men govern their individual conduct and relationships with each other.

Therefore, while American Private Competitive Enterprise is the most productive economic system yet devised, its greater effectiveness is not inherent in or due to the process of capitalism. It is something in America different from Europe and elsewhere that makes our use of tools yield greater results, whether good or bad, in whatever we do.

Let's look at the features that combine to make the economic system in America distinctive and more effective than any other in the world.

First, there is the right of the individual citizen to own property. Regardless of what economic system we have, that right goes further back than the system. It is a vital feature of our complete social, economic and political system.

Second, with the right to own property goes the right of the individual to enter into contract. Having the right to own goods as an individual, I have the parallel right to do as I will with my time and energy as well as with my goods. If I can own goods, I can also dispose of them and keep the proceeds of the transaction. And that means the right to enter into contract.

Third, to exercise either right we must have individual freedom of choice. And individual freedom of choice, in turn, is not necessarily part of an economic system, even though, ultimately there can be no freedom in any one of the several branches of human activity unless there is freedom in all. In any case, the fact of freedom of choice is not necessarily related to the method of production used in an economic system. There can be freedom without capitalism and there can be capitalism without individual freedom. That is to say that the process of production with tools could be carried on under an utter despotism, and men could be free in a society that had no tools or machinery. But both situations are highly improbable.

Moreover, it is no more reasonable to damn our economic system because freedom permits men to abuse their opportunities under that system, than it would be to charge the Church with responsibility for the sins of men who, in exercising that same freedom, refuse to abide by the teachings of the Church.

Freedom is not a right that can be partitioned into a myriad of cubby-holes, allowed in some and denied in others. We are either free or we are not free.

Our rights under freedom carry responsibilities with them, and we set up government to protect those rights, as well as to guard us against harm from persons who would violate our rights through denial of their reciprocal responsibility.

It is important to remember that government did not bestow on us in America the freedom that made us a great country. On the contrary, government was here instituted to protect preexisting rights and responsibilities which our forefathers conceived as coming from God, and to maintain conditions under which people could learn to govern themselves and eventually preserve their rights through self-control.

The benefits resulting from the process of capitalism are much greater when the process is carried on under a system of private competitive enterprise. Government compulsion *could* produce a surplus of goods by lowering the standard of living, save some of the surplus and transform it into tools and machines for the further production of goods. And this could be done without permitting any individual to own property, to receive any profits, or to enter into any contracts on his own volition. *But* the process of capitalism under such conditions would be far less fruitful than under our private competitive system with its private property, right of contract and individual freedom of choice.

It is no less true that the same freedom which unlocks the greatest possibilities for good in our economic system, also permits the evil that men can do in their economic activities.

It is extremely important to recognize freedom itself as the benefactor that multiplies good as well as the culprit that permits the multiplication of evil. Unless we recognize this vital truth we are in constant danger of seeking remedies for our economic ills by destroying the very freedom that makes possible the multiplied blessings of our economic system.

Our problem is to find a solution that will correct the ills without destroying the freedom. We can stop automobile accidents by taking the motors out of cars. But by so doing we would also make the cars useless for transportation. The remedy for the accidents is to improve the individual control and steering of the car, without removing the motor. The same reasoning applies to the removal or correction of our economic ills.

And it is Christianity that gives us the answer.

It was from Christianity that our founding fathers took the idea that authority for custom and law comes from the Supremity of God. Almost half the world today denies God as the supreme Authority for the laws of life, but our founding fathers established a nation on their belief in God as the supreme Ruler of the Universe. They acknowledged Him as the Author and Source of man's inalienable rights, and they recognized the corresponding responsibility of man to God as steward for the freedom God gave him.

Christianity approves private property in the right of the laborer to his hire as well as in its denunciation of theft and covetousness. Nowhere in the Great Book will we find any sustained denial of private property, or the parallel right to enter into private contract.

No less significant is the recognition of individual responsibility, the need as well as the right of the individual to choose for himself.

Even the rich young man could not be saved by the Master alone. He had to *choose*, of his own volition, to be saved. Jesus disagreed, many times, with the ways in which men used what was theirs. He pointed out the consequences of some of the choices they made and offered suggestions as to how men ought to use their property, but He never denied their right to own and use it.

It is to the individual initiative which resulted from the combination of individual freedom, the right to own property and to enter into contract, that we owe the enormous productive capacity of America over other nations.

Thus, Christianity made a great contribution to our economic life by stimulating the process of producing goods with tools provided from profits and savings. This stimulation came from Christian approval of the two broad elements most effective in unleashing and motivating the highest productive powers and capacities of man. These two elements are individual freedom of choice and the right to own property together with the right of contract, and with consequent rights to earnings, profits and investment. The powers resulting from these elements in our economic system are comparable to the motor that makes the automobile go.

In addition to the sanction of freedom and recognition of private property, Christianity makes possible the only controls or steering gear that can direct the power of the incentives without destroying the power itself. It is the control that comes with individual and cooperative acceptance of and obedience to the Ten Commandments and the Two Great Laws of Jesus.

The Ten Commandments, particularly the all-inclusive First Commandment, provide the basis for any sound system of ethics. The laws essential to justice and the realization of self in obedience to God are all there. *In these commandments is contained every principle involved in the functioning of modern economics. They are complete.*

To this provision of criteria or standards for individual conduct in self-interest, Jesus added the law of love for God and our fellowmen. Jesus brought what I like to call the law of "mutuality of interest," as fruition of the law of self-interest in its highest and most effective form. To receive recognition and respect for my rights I must recognize and respect the rights of others, and through that mutual recognition and respect each of us can attain the highest degree of self-realization.

We recognize the need for controls which will protect the rights of all individuals. We can establish those controls entirely through statutory laws which fix the nature and extent of economic relationships and regulate individual conduct. But such laws can be effective only as they limit or remove individual freedom, and thereby defeat the grand purpose of self-realization and development of man through voluntary exercise of his powers and abilities.

The Christian motivated control in private competitive enterprise is definitely superior. Even though it takes longer to effect and is more difficult to realize, it accomplishes the very purpose for which we live. It relies on self-control and obedience to God by an ever increasing number of individuals. Because these are self-motivated on the basis of God's own laws, they finally establish true justice among men coordinately with rising levels of living. It is so that private competitive enterprise accomplishes the grand purpose of self-realization and development of man through voluntary exercise of his powers and abilities.

To the extent that the laws of Moses and the laws of Jesus are accepted and obeyed by men they become the common denominator of faith which guides our choices in action. That faith provides the sanctions for custom and legal code, and inspires voluntary obedience to the government which bases its administration on those same sanctions in maintaining tranquility and promoting the general welfare.

With Christianity so implemented we shall pass through the transition of force in government, to voluntary obedience in response to divine will. An economic system becomes the hand-maiden of religion.

The advantages and evils that arise in the operation of our economic system come from the same source, the conduct of people who live under the system. There *are* selfish people who exploit others in many walks of life, social, political and even religious, as well as economic. We *can* be stupidly ignorant and make mistakes, as well as commit sins that injure other persons. But the remedy for these ills is to correct and improve the people, individual by individual, and lift the standards by which they live, not to change our economic system. Modifying our economic system to prevent bad behavior is to destroy the very freedom under which people make mistakes and commit sin.

But, neither must we destroy the incentive that results from inequality. It is inequality, the constant search and effort for adjustment, emulation, improvement of one's status or condition, to lift one's self to higher levels, that brings motion and progress, and keeps life alive.

An ocean without motion, stilled by utter equality, would be a vast, stagnant pool, smothered in the miasma of rotting things and death.

Shall we, in deference to equality, cease our efforts to excel, for betterment and to make ourselves more worthy? Shall we lessen our efforts in performing stewardship, in order to wait for those who lag behind or refuse to get started? Must we let them catch up with us before we make further efforts? Or shall we welcome the challenge of inequality and each of us furnish the example that will challenge and encourage our less ambitious brothers to improve themselves?

I think the questions provide their own answers.

In our struggle to achieve self-control and universal acceptance of the laws of God as the standards for individual and national conduct, as well as the improvement of man as the way to remedy our ills, we need not rely on our own strength alone.

Through faith in God and obedience to His laws we become heirs to a wisdom and strength infinitely greater than our own. We grow in grace as fulfilment follows the use of our gifts in the building of His kingdom.

We are all human beings. The problems we face are finally those of establishing and maintaining effectively coordinated relationships with each other. It is only as our method of economic control helps us to become better and abler, more understanding and cooperative as individual human beings, that it can serve the dual purpose of preserving the benefits of freedom even as it protects us against the mis-use of that freedom. Both control and the acceptance of its limitations must be voluntary.

That is the contribution of Christianity to our American system of Private Competitive Enterprise, and the challenge to those who are so fortunate as to live under the system.

CHAPTER 3

THE FALLACY OF THE MIDDLE WAY

IT is a fashion of the day in professional educational circles and even among religious leaders to advocate revolutionary change in approaching our economic and related problems. They indulge now and then in ill-concealed contempt for the "reactionaries" who refuse to modify or repudiate traditional premises, as well as for the radicals who promise the impossible without regard for the teachings of experience. Many of them lean toward the radicals but are less radical.

It may have been in something of this spirit, as well as actuated by a genuine desire to solve problems which perplex the best of us, that the World Council of Churches, meeting in Amsterdam, Holland, from August 22nd to September 4 of 1948, made its recommendation for a middle way between communism and capitalism. It is because of the prestige of this organization that its recommendation is here considered.

Having pointed out what they believe to be points of conflict between Christianity and Communism on the one hand, and Christianity and Capitalism on the other, those in attendance at the meeting stated: (page 45 of report)

"The Christian Churches should reject the ideologies of both communism and laissez-faire capitalism, and should seek to draw men away from the false assumption that these extremes are the only alternatives. Each has made promises which it could not redeem. Communist ideology puts emphasis on economic justice, and promises that freedom will come automatically after the completion of the revolution. Capitalism puts the emphasis upon freedom, and promises that justice will follow as a by-product of free enterprise; that, too, is an ideology which has proved false. It is the responsibility of Christians to seek new, creative solutions which never allow either justice or freedom to destroy each other."

The report speaks wisely as it continues: "The greatest contribution that the Church can make to the renewal of society is for it

189

(the Church) to be renewed in its own life in faith and obedience to its Lord." With this statement I find myself in accord. And I am just as certain that an honest and unbiased effort to renew "the life of the Church in faith and obedience to its Lord," as the Christians seek "new and creative solutions which never allow either justice or freedom to destroy each other," would lead to solutions far afield from any middle-way alternative as is in effect proposed in the report from Amsterdam.

For example, it is an error to think of justice and freedom as antagonistic to each other, even though the method of search for either may be contradictory to the other. Indeed, the two terms have so much in common as to be almost interchangeable with each other. Surely, it is not just to destroy freedom, nor can we remain free without justice. Neither is really possible without the other. It is only through a misconception of freedom as untrammelled license, which it is not, or of justice as disregard for individual rights, which it is not, that either can be regarded as destroying the other.

The recommendation of the World Council of Churches, in spite of its manifest sincerity and good intentions, is dangerous and, taken seriously, would defeat its purpose if actually put into effect. That is because the authors of the report, in their confusion of terms and failure to understand the real conflict having its outward semblance in the battle between so-called communism and capitalism, evade the real issue that must be settled.

Let us first dispose of the confusion occasioned by the use of the term "laissez-faire capitalism" as used in the quotations above. It is the only place in the report where the term is used, and is said to have been used there to placate Charles Taft, who objected to the sweeping denunciation of capitalism. But the capitalism meant in that statement is exactly the same capitalism referred to anywhere else in the report. We do not have laissez-faire capitalism and the proponents of capitalism do not advocate it now any more than they did fifty years ago.

I am aware that foreign delegates to the council meeting were thinking of "capitalism" as they have known it in Europe. But when American proponents of the council report disseminate the attack on "capitalism" here in America they do not point out that the report is aimed at something else than we have here at home. It is against our own economic system that they hurl the denunciations and recommendations of the World Council of Churches.

Capitalism as it exists here is something different from what the writers of the World Council of Churches report had in mind. That capitalism, as it actually exists, is not an ideology, even though it is spoken of as such. It is only a process which is widely used in an economic system, under an ideology of freedom and the recognition of private property in production goods as well as others. Capitalism does not promise that justice will follow as a by-product of free enterprise. Capitalism promises only that the products of past industry, transferred into tools and machinery, guided by management, will increase the production of goods through the more effective use of human energy and time on natural resources. And that is all it promises or can promise.

The criticism hurled against capitalism should rightly be hurled against freedom and the religious faith and sanctions on which we rely for reasonable and just behavior from men living under the ideology of freedom and private property.

The real issue or alternative is not between communism and capitalism. It is rather between paganism and Christianity.

It is not good thinking to place an ideology or religion as an alternative at one extreme and an economic process at the opposite extreme. For communism is an ideology, really a religion, which controls an economic process using the products of past industry for the further production of goods as part of its control over the entire life of a people. The same process of using products of past industry to produce more goods is controlled in America by individual initiative and voluntary cooperation within the limits of a constitution and laws passed for the mutual protection of individual rights.

So, to be fair, the comparison might be made between communism and the American system of freedom and private property, as ideologies. Or it might be between the religions that are the real sanctions behind both methods of control.

Freedom and private property are tied inexorably with Christianity. Christianity may well be said to be the religion of freedom and private property. And freedom can no more be separated from individual responsibility to God than can private property. Certainly, it was Christianity that, more than any other religion the world has yet known, set out to make man free. It was Goethe who pointed out to us that "we are made free . . . by revering something that is above us. For by revering it we rise to its level, and by our recognition attest the fact that we ourselves bear within us the germ of the higher existence and are worthy of matching it."

The highest freedom is that of self-realization through the use of free choice and opportunity to make our lives harmonize with the Will of God as that Will is implemented in the laws that govern life. And the core of the truth under Christianity is that obedience to God, through which we harmonize our lives with the Eternal, is and must always be voluntary, the result of deliberate choice. Therein are we free.

On the other hand, there is just as inexorable a relationship between communism and paganism. From the teachings of Karl Marx down through the declarations and actual policies and programs of communism, particularly as developed in Russia and now setting the pattern for world communism, the initial and basic premise is denial of God. In place of the Eternal God of the Christian, the communist has a number of idols, chief among which is Joseph Stalin. It is a pagan religion dedicated to the worship of materialism and enforced through the rule of man over other men. Obedience to the religion is involuntary within the society where it is in force. Under communism men worship the creature rather than the Creator.

So we have on one hand the economic system mistakenly called Capitalism, which is really a system of freedom and private property, called competitive private enterprise, and depending upon the moral sanctions of Christianity to guide and improve men living under the system. The ideology is Americanism. The religion is Christianity. The process of production is capitalism. Government is by law.

On the other hand we have an economic system called Communism, which also uses the processes of Capitalism, but relies on a different set of sanctions to guide and control the process and the conduct of men. The ideology is Communism. The religion is Paganism. Government is by men.

Therefore the real issue confronted by the World Council of Churches, and by all of us can be stated in either of two ways. The alternatives are:

AMERICANISM VERSUS COMMUNISM

OR

CHRISTIANITY VERSUS PAGANISM

But the basic issue is Christianity verus Paganism, or Jesus of Nazareth versus Karl Marx of Germany, the Son of God versus the apostle of atheism. It is really to settle that issue that the world is breaking into flames of what may be a third and perhaps final world war within two generations.

The error of the World Council of Churches lay in suggesting that a middle way must be found between two religions or ideologies rather than between two methods of implementing the same religion or ideology.

I think all of us would agree that there can be compromise in the way of applying or activating the same truth, for then one need not compromise the truth or principle itself. But, there can be no compromise on basic principle without destroying the principle itself. And here the basic principle is the first and most fundamental commandment of them all: "I am the Lord thy God; thou shalt have no other Gods before me."

The fallacy of the middle way as a "new, creative solution" for the "renewal of society," as proposed in the World Council of Churches report and as concurred in by many of our clergy, lies in the fact that there can be no compromise or middle way between God and the denial of God in materialism. One believes or does not believe. There is no middle way of partial belief in God and partial denial of God as the Creator and Ruler of all. Shall we venture to point out wherein Jesus was right and Marx was wrong, or wherein Marx was right and Jesus was wrong, and accept the compromise as our faith?

Even though we can legitimately seek a middle way between extreme alternatives in methods of applying a basic principle, or in seeking to accomplish a given purpose, we must still be careful in the choice of method, lest the method we choose lead to abandonment of the very principle or purpose we would serve.

The communists in America and elsewhere have been diabolically clever in identifying their social objectives, justice, brotherhood and the rest, with those of the Christian Church. Through such identification they have succeeded in joining forces in a common attack on what they call "capitalism" and setting up as a remedy for that "capitalism" increasing power in government for the socialization of economic activity. The naive exponent of reform sees in Federal Aid only a charitable distribution of the total capacity for help to the places where it is most needed. He fails to see in the method used a building up of centralized power which must eventually substitute the State for God.

Well might Earl Browder, leading American-born disciple of Marx and one-time head of the American communist party, boast of how his party had invaded the church groups of America:

> "It is significant that the communist party, more than any other group, has been able to achieve successful united fronts with church groups on the most important issues of the day. This is not due to any compromise on our part with religion as such. In going among the religious masses we are for the first time able to bring our anti-religious ideas to them."

By yielding to the lure of communist promises and methods and being misled to attack the process of producing goods as the evil instead of attacking our laxity in moral sanctions in the lives of those who live under our economic system, many a churchman has actually become an ally of communism in the ultimate destruction of Christianity as the sanction behind and the power in economic life.

Through use of the principle of lesser concessions, inducing their victims to accept one step after another, each of little consequence in itself, but in the aggregate taking us all of the way, the communist and his fellow-traveller have induced thousands of people to look to socialism or some form of collective control as the answer to our economic ills. This same collective control becomes the middle-way, or a step on the way to totalitarianism.

Regardless of the beautiful things said and the fascinating mirage held up to our over-anxious and impatient souls, we dare not ignore the ugly truth that behind the collective methods, with constant growing of centralized power of government over men, socialism continues to creep into our lives and must eventually substitute the State for God as the arbiter of what is right or wrong, good or bad, ultimately accomplish the triumph of paganism over Christianity as the common denominator of faith and relationship among men.

If men could know that the alternatives offered as extremes between which they seek a middle way, were really extremes between which there can be no compromise, they would seek the remedies for our economic and social ills where they are to be found instead of being drawn into a compromise between faith and atheism. For we know that any compromise in faith is the first step toward its betrayal.

When men propose to find a cure for the ills growing out of freedom and private property, by finding a middle way or compromise between capitalism and communism, whether or not they know it, they are really asking for a middle way between Christianity and paganism.

And I say there can be no compromise between paganism and Christianity. To seek a middle way between the two is like unto breaking bread with the devil in the shadow of the cross.

We must find a solution that will preserve both justice and freedom, let them live together without mutual destruction at the hands of their proponents. We must bring about in society a renewal of the virtues without which no society can be sound or long endure.

To that challenge my answer is to offer Christianity itself as the solution. We already have the answer at hand, if we will use it. Our problem is to find a way to induce men to live by those principles.

CHAPTER 4

A PRACTICAL CHRISTIAN FORMULA

THERE is no easy road to redemption of the individual and correction of the economic ills that result from the mistakes and sins of human beings. But there is a sure road, a road that builds us as we go and points the way to fulfillment for the divine purpose in the life of man.

Christianity is the answer. It is practical religion, down to earth with its truths reaching to the skies. It is not an impossible ideal as is sometimes taught, but a philosophy and faith through which men can achieve the utmost within the limits of their capacities.

Truth is universal. The principles which Jesus taught and approved are sound in whatever aspect of life they may be applied. The psalmist caught that truth when he pointed out that the wise man seeks to understand the "law of the Lord," meditates on that law day and night until he knows it and sees its application in every phase of life. And so, understanding, he is like a tree by the rivers of water, that bringeth forth his fruit in his season, whose leaf does not wither, and who prospers in whatsoever he does.

If you have the basic truths of life, you will find that they apply in whatever you do or wherever you are. Mastering them in one branch of human activity, you have the key to understanding in every other. That is as close as we can come to the "Open Sesame" that man has sought through the ages.

The doctor, the lawyer, the dentist, the business man, the preacher, teacher, engineer, salesman, truck driver, mechanic, musician, whatever may be the calling in which a man seeks success, accomplishes a greater measure of achievement if he is a Christian in practice. But what we want is more than a Christian *as a business man;* we want a Christian business man, who carries his business on *as a Christian.* And so with the rest.

I know, there are many who do not believe that success in business or profession is possible if one follows the teachings of Christianity. Those who believe profit contrary to service or use, who deplore self-interest as a motivation of conduct, are prone to shake their heads at the mere suggestion that Christianity and economic success are compatible. But they are mistaken, for stewardship in one field is just as important as in another. The laws that govern responsibility are not limited to certain narrow fields of altruistic endeavor, nor do they deny rewards of success to any who are faithful in their stewardship, no matter what the field of activity.

If it is true, as sometimes is alleged by professional Christians, that the principles of business (or American private competitive enterprise with its profit motive) are in conflict with or opposed to the principles of Christianity, then it follows that we must either give up the practices and benefits of business in order to be Christians and so save our souls, or we must give up Christianity in order not to revert to primitive economics and days of the caveman in our standards of living. The remaining alternative would be to adopt socialism, establish a constantly centralizing government and increasing control over the economic life of the people, until freedom is gone and the state takes the place of God as the arbiter of what is good or bad, right or wrong.

Our problem is to discover how one can succeed as a Christian in economic life.

What are the universal principles that can guide us to successful achievement? Is there a formula in which we can express the essence of what Christianity has to offer as criteria for our conduct? That is very important to me, for when I find those principles I am going to risk my life on them. I cannot afford to be mistaken. Nor does it help to listen to many voices, for they speak in many languages and offer a wide variety of answers. I cannot be sure that they mean well by me, for the Pied Piper has had many relatives and descendants.

But I can begin with faith in the Book that men have revered and followed for centuries. I can look into the nature of things as they are and find revelations of the Will that I seek to obey. I can expose myself to the spirit that has come into the lives of countless men before me.

And so doing, it has come to me that the essence of what Christianity has to offer me may be expressed in three basic principles, all of them premised on the one great commandment, "Thou shalt have no other Gods before me."

I call these three principles my three-legged stool. I make it a three-legged stool because I know that a stool with three legs will stand firmly on any ground, no matter how rough or rugged. I have tried standing on this stool and have learned that it stands, and that I can build safely and soundly on its foundation.

The first leg is this: "Ye shall know the truth, and the truth will make you free." This is as practical a promise as man was ever given. Quite aside from its origin and specialized meaning in the complete text, the statement is one of hard common sense, applicable to any problem or project. Before we can even begin operations we should know the facts. The engineer should know the nature of the soil and sub-soil before he builds a bridge or road. He must have the facts of projected use of a building before he designs it, and must have the data regarding materials and a myriad of other facts, before he can safely estimate what the building should be or what it will cost.

The doctor must understand anatomy, have the truth, the facts concerning human beings before he dares to make decisions that will affect their physical condition. The industrialist needs facts regarding markets, sources of supply and the rest, before he goes ahead with a program of production and sales. The politician should understand many things and deal with true facts before he legislates for the regulation or control of any activity. In whatever field or branch it may be, no man can reach a sound decision or build a right policy unless first he has the facts.

Here we meet a tremendous obstacle. What often passes for truth and fact as a basis for action is no more than a rationalization of reasons to justify what has been pre-decided. When we are told to seek the truth, it is meant that we should seek to know all the truth available and applicable to the problem or situation, and that we should accept that truth even when we do not like it.

It is through inculcation of respect for truth and honest consideration of fact that we can correct and even prevent the unhappy fallacies which, in turn, lead millions of people to believe things that are not true. This must finally be our answer to the naive and futile quest of something for nothing, or the tearing down of the industrious to lift the indigent. Here is the first step to correct the fallacies discussed in Part Three.

The second leg of the stool comes from the same place that the first came from. It is this: "Do ye unto others as you would have others do unto you."

That may be discounted as an impractical and visionary ideal. But it is utterly practical, sound and realistic. The principle is the basis of all selling and of effective human relationships. Let me illustrate out of my own experience.

Years ago I was sales manager for a manufacturer of beds, springs and mattresses. I was given the job in a strange way, the result of making a speech to our sales force gathered together informally one Sunday afternoon. The President of our company was sitting on the other side of a partition with no roof, discharging his current sales manager, while I was making my speech. He apparently stopped to listen to me. At any rate, when the speech was done, I was sales manager of the company.

I had never been a sales manager before, nor had I ever sold beds, springs and mattresses. I had come into the organization as a research economist. So I had to learn. Part of my learning was to visit retail furniture stores to see how they handled our goods. It was on one of these trips that I met the glorious red-head who introduced me to the golden rule in selling.

When I walked into the store where she came up to meet me, I asked for a certain mattress which we manufactured. She looked at me pityingly and said gently that they were running a high-grade store, with a fine clientele, and handled only the best merchandise. Then she proceeded to sell me a hair mattress. I shall not enter into the relative merits of our mattress and the hair mattress, but, that woman was so good that I might have gone back to the office with a vermin shelter on my back if I had not got out in time.

When I returned to the office and told my story to the Chief, he asked me what I proposed to do about it. And then came the great idea. "Let's hire her!" I exclaimed. "If she can do that to me, when I am on guard, I wonder what she would do to anyone who had not yet made up his mind on what he wanted to buy. Maybe she can teach retail salesmen to sell our stuff." So we hired her, to go out to retailers all over the country and demonstrate to salesmen how furnitue, particularly mattresses, should be sold. She stayed in each place two weeks and before long we had a number of women, as rapidly as they could be found and trained, to do the same thing.

It paid well. Our sales of mattresses rose rapidly and a tremendous fund of good-will began to develop in the stores. What happened, and what I had not realized when the idea came to me, was that we were doing for the retailer what we would like to have done for us if we were the retailers. We modified our sales policy with less emphasis on the selling of goods and more on the giving of service. Our salesmen were asked to find ways and means to help the retailer sell the goods he had already bought, and then he would buy more and more of them. The policy worked. And the promotion cost was really low, slightly over 7% on the increase of sales for the first six months after the visit.

During World War II, I served for several years as a panel member for one of the war-labor boards. It was an interesting experience and taught me that the way to get what one wants is to want what one ought to get. In short, I made it my business to seek the right answers, not merely the answers I was expected to find. After all, these men, whose representatives were either trying to get more money or better conditions for them, even in time of war, or who were trying to stay in business in spite of the difficulties and sometimes unreasonable demands made on them from various directions, all needed to work together for a common purpose. They had genuine interests in common, and my job, as I saw it, was to help them work in harmony and in their common interest.

It is tremendously significant, I think, that of all the cases on which I served, there was not one that needed to come before the board, if only each side had treated the other side as it would like to be treated if it were the other side. Most of the troubles in industrial relations, although not all of them, could be prevented by an honest application of the Golden Rule by both sides within the organization itself.

The same rule would go far in a short time, to break down the barriers that now hold many employers and employees apart and prevent them from recognizing their common interests as fellow-workers in serving the customer.

Here we have the effective remedy for unfair competition, the greed and avarice that are largely responsible for the evils of materialism charged mistakenly against our American capitalistic system. No one quarrels with baseball or football because the scores are uneven and one side or the other wins the game. We do want the rules to be fair and impartially administered. And then, if each side treats the other as itself asks to be treated under the rules, we get a fair game with full incentive for each player to do his best, win or lose.

The same reasoning holds true in economic competition. Fair play is a far better solution than deliberately handicapping the better players or manipulating the score to make the game come out even.

The third leg of the stool is not quite so easy to accept, but is the most important of the three, for it provides the motivation for human cooperation in the common task of increasing the usefulness of natural resources. It is: *"Love ye one another even as I have loved you."*

There is a sound psychological reason for this rule. It reaches even further than the second leg of the stool, because it provides a reason for doing unto others as we would have them do unto us. Both, taken together, give us the complete law of mutuality of interest, which is the fruition of the basic law of self-preservation in its highest and most effective form.

The way in which it works is simple. Whether or not we like it, most people do not believe us because of our faultless logic or overwhelming evidence of fact. These are important and even vitally necessary, but the fact remains that most people believe and trust the people whom they like. The politician knows that, and sometimes overdoes it. But it is still true that the way to get most folks to believe you and trust you is to get them to like you. It is not an infallible rule, but it works in the vast majority of cases.

And the way to get folks to like you is to like them! Just as simple as that.

However, the effort is futile if not sincere. I could make up my mind that I wanted you to like me. But the effort would fail if it were deliberate. Insincerity and artificiality would defeat the effort. The rule works best when he who uses it is not aware that he is doing so. Suppose you get up in the morning, glad just to be alive, remind yourself of all the fine people you know, the people with whom you work. Think on the joy and privilege of being with them, how much you owe them for the kind things they have done to you. Forget the evil and unhappy things you have suffered as being no more than the results of mistakes made by people who meant better.

In whatever way you do it, approach your work with a glow of friendliness in your heart for your fellow men. And you won't need to use any tricks, devices or subterfuges to win men. They will feel your love for them and, in spite even of existing ill-will, in time will respond with love for you.

It may be an over-simple formula. Certainly it omits many details and requirements that others will deem important. It is perhaps no more than a beginning. But I do know that it works. And it is far better to get started actually applying the teachings, than to wait for the perfect answer that will always work and suit everyone. I shall welcome such an answer if and when it comes. In the mean-time, I am glad to know that my three-legged stool gives me some-thing very solid and substantial on which to build my life.

The three legs taken together will contribute greatly toward build-ing the individual and national character, to make our people fit for freedom.

Instead of destroying freedom in quest of socially determined justice, or justice in quest of uncontrolled freedom, by setting up collectivistic controls over our economic life, we can achieve the ultimately automatic controls that Christianity provides by helping men to make themselves fit for the responsibilities of self-develop-ment. Government serves as the referee over a contest in which individuals vie with each other for self-realization and the most effective use of their capacities for stewardship, rather than as the tyrant who decides who shall have what.

It is true that there must be leadership as we learn to be fit for freedom. Leadership must articulate for the group. But that leader-ship must ever be subject, with the people themselves, to the God of all, whose eternal wisdom provides the sanctions behind custom and law. Otherwise the leadership, once intrenched, could lead us to the very dictatorship through totalitarian government to which Chris-tianity offers the only adequate protest and antidote.

Perhaps, the failure of mankind to benefit as it should by the truths revealed by the Almighty, points to the need for a miracle to get these truths fully accepted now. Well, miracles still happen when unfaltering faith is united with untiring work.

To invoke the miracle of making the formula work in places where men are governed by doubt, to provide the courage, fortitude and persistence needed to stick to the task and actually get it done, I add two vitally necessary ingredients to my Christian prescription.

The first is faith. It is true that faith can move mountains. The story books are replete with records of men whose invincible faith turned disheartening defeat into ultimate victory. Without faith we cannot live; with faith we can make ourselves invincible.

The other ingredient is work. Faith and work can make the miracle, now even as they have all through the centuries. Through faith and work we can overcome obstacles, solve our problems and achieve fulfilment. There is no substitute for either, no matter how far we carry technology in the greater utilization of human effort and time on natural resources.

Faith, in the spirit of the Master, wins salvation through work. Both are universals in religion. And it is the universals in religion that draw men together in cooperation for their common good. It is the hair-splitting trivialities that set men against each other and bring about the tyranny of minorities.

"He that overcometh shall inherit all things; and I will be his God and he shall be my son."

CHAPTER 5

WALKING WITH GOD

I am no theologian, nor am I interested in dissensions over the relative importance of gospels and epistles, prophets or apostles. I am not concerned in ultimately trivial deliberations of the denominations, nor do I care how many angels can dance on the point of a needle.

I do know that I am in dire need of something to live by, through which I may seek and attain fulfilment.

I have faith that the God who could create a universe and provide for the government of that universe through the implementation of His will in natural law, can no less create in me the capacity to reach and receive even without the intervention of other men. I need only Him and no less than Him can satisfy my need.

Whether I be in the desert, staggering blindly under the heat of a merciless sun; or in the fastness of a mountain, locked in its rocky walls; or buried in the depths of a primal forest; though I be lost in crowds or all alone with only the murmur of the stars to comfort me; God is there, waiting to walk with me.

But to know Him is not a power that springs from within me, the spontaneous generation of spirit from matter, the synthesis of understanding from a crucible of science, or the triumph of will in self-instituted vision.

If, like the earth-bound smoke of an unacceptable sacrifice, words tumble from my lips but fail to rise to heaven; if the sound of my voice seems to fall on deaf ears, or is only an echo in an empty cavern, it is because I have not yet learned to find my way to God. Mine is not yet the gift of awareness through which He makes Himself known to me and helps me to feel His presence.

How can I have the gift of awareness? Are there measurable and determinative steps by which I can make this gift mine?

I do not know.

But I do know that I can relax my stubborn resistance to revelation. I can relinquish my will to the Almighty and meditate on His goodness and mercy. I can yield Him my utter obedience and welcome the tuning of my soul to the soul of the Infinite. And I can do this wherever or whatever I happen to be.

I can open my heart to Him in prayer, not to ask for gift or boon, or to make my burdens light, but to yield myself without qualification, asking only: "Thy Will be done."

Having seen the evidence of His might and all-pervading spirit in the nature of all that is, I can have the faith of young Samuel, hearing a voice in the night and rising to answer with his trembling "Here am I, Lord. Speak; for Thy servant heareth." Mine can be the courage to seek understanding of His doctrine through obedience to His will. And God creates in me the gift I seek!

In the wake of the gift of awareness, there is made available to me the power men have sought feverishly in the by-paths of faith. The strength beyond my own strength, which has always been there waiting for release, pours through me in a flood of understanding.

How do I know? How can you know?

Have you ever found yourself in the presence of difficulties and obstacles that stood like a stone wall in your path, when you saw no way around and lacked the strength to go through; when you were worn out, tired unto death and knew not where to turn for help?

I have stood in such a spot, ont once but often. I have learned that I can reach out and ask for strength. If my faith be great, strength comes to me. I do not know just how or from where, nor can I prove from Whom. I only know that strength comes and I can go on again.

I have gone to bed at night with a problem I could not solve. My tired brain, exhausted from gyrations of thought, shrinking from another single effort, has been glad to lay the problem aside while I asked quietly for understanding, for help to find the right answer. And again, if my faith be serene I can sleep. It does not always work, but more often than not, when morning comes the answer comes with morning. It is not always the answer I thought I wanted, for my desire may be at fault and I must do that which is right. But, my prayer is answered.

Think of the enormous power wrapped up in the atomic bomb! Science has found a way to contain an unmeasurable amount of compressed energy in an incomprehensibly small space, with frightful power to destroy. Yet the atomic bomb, compared to the invisible power that is God, is as insignificant as a moment compared to eternity. And this power is ours, not to command, but to petition. We win it through faith and obedience.

Where faith is great, so also is that which is given to us.

I cannot prove that to you. You must believe or not believe, as you choose. I can only give you the answer of the blind man who was given his sight in faith by the Master and then bedevilled by those who sought to destroy his benefactor. They scouted and scoffed at his story of moistened dust and washing it off his eyes at the Pool of Siloam. And, at last, weary of their heckling, the man who had been blind turned on his tormentors. Not pretending to understand what they were trying to do to him, nor even attempting to explain what had happened to him, he gave them the perfect answer, the word that comes from one who has risen through faith to those who have not yet learned to believe:

"One thing I know, that, whereas I was blind, now I see."

GOD SPEAKS

The silence of the Night
Throbs and pulses on my heart,
Like some wild thing
That cannot speak;
But makes its presence known and felt
By means that need no voice or cry
To bear its message through the night.

'Tis so that God can speak:
Lay His hand upon my heart
And still the doubts
That hover there;
I need no ear to hear His voice
Nor sight to know His presence near,
Within the stillness of His might.

READING LIST

A reference list from which the student can supplement his readings on the reconciliation of religion and economics and related problems. Those which should be of special interest are marked with an asterisk (*).

Bach, Marcus. *Report to Protestants.* Indianapolis: The Bobbs-Merrill Company, 1948.

*Bell, Bernard Iddings. *God Is Not Dead.* New York: Harper and Brothers, 1945.

Borth, Christy. *Pioneers of Plenty.* Indianapolis: The Bobbs-Merrill Company, 1942.

*Brogan, Colm. *Our New Masters.* London: Hollis and Carter, 1948.

*Budenz, Louis F. *The Cry Is Peace.* Chicago: Henry Regnery Company, 1952.

*Carrel, Dr. Alexis. *Prayer.* New York: Morehouse-Gorham Co., 1948.

Cassel, G. *From Protectionism through Planned Economy.* Cobden Memorial Lecture; London, 1934.

Christian Economics. A Periodical for the Clergy published by the Christian Freedom Foundation, Inc.: 36 West 58th Street, New York 19, N. Y.

*Clark and Rimanoczy. *How We Live.* New York: D. Van Nostrand Company, Inc., 1949.

Communist International: *Blueprint for World Conquest.* Intro. by William Henry Chamberlin. Human Events: Washington and Chicago, 1946.

*Cross, Richard, Editor. *The God That Failed.* Confessions of six outstanding reformed Communists. New York: Harper and Brothers, 1949.

Crow, Carl. *The Great American Customer.* New York: Harper and Brothers, 1943.

*Daton, William. *Shirtsleeve Economics.* New York: Appleton-Century-Crofts, Inc., 1952.

Drummond, Henry. *Natural Law in the Spiritual World.* Philadelphia: Henry Altemus Company.

Faith and Freedom. Monthly Journal of Spiritual Mobilization: 1521 Wilshire Blvd., Los Angeles 17, Calif.

Flynn, John T. *The Road Ahead.* New York: The Devin-Adair Company, 1949.

*Gide and Rist. *A History of Economic Doctrines.* Boston: D. C. Heath & Co., 1948.

Goethe. *Wisdom and Experience.* Selections by Ludwig Curtius. New York: Pantheon Books, Inc., 1949.

*Goodspeed, Edgar J. *A Life of Jesus.* New York: Harper & Brothers, 1950.

*Graebner, Theodore. *The Business Man and The Church.* Clinton, S. C.: The Jacobs Press, 1942.

Graham, F. D. *Social Goals and Economic Institutions.* Princeton: Princeton University Press, 1942.

Harper, F. A. *Liberty. A Path to Its Recovery.* Irvington-on-Hudson: New York: The Foundation for Economic Education, 1949.

Hayek, Friedrich A. *The Road to Serfdom.* Chicago: University of Chicago Press, 1944.

*Hazlitt, Henry. *Economics in One Lesson.* Rockefeller Center, N. Y.: Pocket Books, Inc., 1948.

Hitler, Adolf. *Mein Kampf.* New York: Reynal & Hitchcock, 1939.

Holy Bible.

*Kiekhofer, William H. *Economic Principles, Problems and Policies.* New York: D. Appleton-Century Company, 1936.

LaMott, Robert L. *The Conservation of Freedom.* New York: The Exposition Press, 1949.

*Lane, Rose Wilder. *Give Me Liberty.* New York: Longmans, Green and Co., 1936.

Liebman, Joshua Loth. *Peace of Mind.* New York: Simon and Schuster, 1946.

*Link, Henry C. *The Way to Security.* Garden City, N. Y.: Doubleday & Company, 1951.

*Lippmann, Walter. *The Good Society.* Boston: Little, Brown and Company, 1941.

Lutz, Harley L. *A Platform for the American Way.* New York: Appleton-Century-Crofts, Inc., 1952.

MacArthur, Gen. Douglas. *Revitalizing a Nation.* Chicago: The Heritage Foundation, Inc., 1952.

*Manion, Clarence. *The Key to Peace.* Chicago: The Heritage Foundation, Inc., 1951.

*Mises, Ludwig von. *Human Action.* New Haven: Yale University Press, 1949.

*Morrison, A. Cressy. *Man Does Not Stand Alone.* New York: Fleming H. Revell Company, 1944.

Mussolini, Benito. *The Doctrine of Fascism.* Florence: Vallecchi.

Mussolini, Benito. *The Corporate State.* Florence: Vallecchi.

Noüy, Lecomte du. *Human Destiny.* New York: Longmans, Green and Co., 1947.

Oxman, G. Bromley. *The Ethical Ideals of Jesus in a Changing World.* New York: Abingdon-Cokesbury Press.

*Peale, Norman Vincent. *A Guide to Confident Living.* New York: Prentice-Hall, Inc., 1948.

Queeny, Edgar M. *The Spirit of Enterprise.* New York: Scribners, 1943.

Randall, Clarence B. *A Creed for Free Enterprise.* Boston: Little, Brown & Company, 1952.

*Snyder, Carl. *Capitalism the Creator.* New York: The Macmillan Company, 1940.

Sorokin, P. A. *The Crisis of Our Age.* New York: E. P. Dutton and Co., Inc., 1942.

*Spencer, Herbert. *The Man versus The State.* Caldwell, Idaho: The Caxton Printers, Ltd., 1944.

Volpe, Gioacchino. *History of the Fascist Movement.* Edizioni Di Nouvissima: Roma A. XIV (1935).

*Watts, V. Orval. *Away from Freedom.* Los Angeles: The Foundation for Social Research.

*Weaver, Henry G. *Mainspring.* Detroit: Talbot Books, 1947.

*World Council of Churches. *Report on First Assembly; Amsterdam, Holland:* August 22 to September 4, 1948. World Council of Churches, 297 Fourth Avenue, New York City.

INDEX

Profit, a "more," 120, 122; added utility, 49; amount debatable, 122; basic concept, 119; consists of utility, 119; control of, 123; defined, 45-6; destruction means civilization loss, 51; difference in esteem, 83; economic concept, 121; error in conception, 45; genesis of civilization, 123; hope for,
44; in enterprise, 120-1; income tax taken from, 121; inducement to enterprise, 123; limits of, 99; maximum benefit, 124; necessary to production,
123; out of surplus, 120; payment for risk, 46; payment, for use of capital,
110; for use of tools, 99; product of tools, 49; production, 37; reward
for human beings, 102; reward for service, 45; risk greater than rent or
interest, 116; share decreases over time, 122; social concept, 121; urge to
enterprise, 123; why can be paid, 121; why must be paid, 121; why to
both parties, 83
Profit and loss system, 45
Profit motive, 43; fallacy in criticism, 44-5; factor in price changes, 88; mistaken for avarice, 43; motor in auto, 46; power in economics, 46; rooted
in self-preservation, 15
Progressive tax, 159
Property, controlled by state, 129; under Christian Socialists, 131; under
Communism, 133; under Fascism, 135; under Nazism, 136; under Social-
ism, 130-2; under Socialist-Labor, 137
Property, essential to sovereignty, 130; individual right to own, 183
Property, private, abolished under anarchy, 143; approved by Christianity, 185;
protection encourages saving, 59; tied with freedom and Christianity, 191-
2; under Fascism, 135
Prosperity, under American enterprise, 181
Psalmist, rich promise, 196
Public, Mr. John Q., 160
Purchasing power through character, 69
Purpose, holds world together, 18, 19; in economic life, 125, 126; in the
universe, 6

Quantity of matter and force remains the same, 48, 49

Rabbits and fish, 32
Reciprocal relationships in exchange, 169-70
Redeemable, in gold, 65
Redemption, no easy road, 196; through stewardship, 176-7
Red-head saleswoman, 199
Regimentation to stop depression, 168
Religion, conflict with economics, 3; defined, 1, 3; fundamentals and trivialities,
151; no compromise with atheism, 193; origin of, 3, 4; practice, 9, 196-
203; roots on control, 127; subject to criticisms against capitalism, 191;
two root ideas, 3, 4; universals, 203
Rent, amount paid, 121; can and must be paid, 118-9; compared with interest,
118; defined, 117; for use of capital goods, 117; includes depreciation
and care, 118; limits of, 99; payment to human beings, 102; payment
for use of capital, 110, 117; risk different than for interest, 116
Reprieve, under Eisenhower, 141
Republic, constitutional, dangerous changes, 146; best form of individualism
government, 144; strength, 145; weakness, 145
Republican Party, slim margin of power, 141
Responsibility, individual, 185-6; inseparable from freedom, 17

Webb, Sidney and Beatrice, 137
Welfare, the road to socialism in U. S., 139
Welfare state, England, 137; Eisenhower a reprieve, 141; in U. S., 139; unscrambling, 141
Wisdom, heirs to, 188; in faith, 20; no monopoly, 151-2; sanctions from God, 202
Work, or labor, in production, 33; wins salvation in faith, 203
Workers, account for 85% of cost, 54; dependent on pay-rolls, 104; employment dilemma, 107; exploit other workers, 53-4, 101; how affect standard of living, 53; not entitled to profits, 103; victims of unproductive wage-increases, 100-1; who are, 101; see also, Labor
World Council of Churches, Amsterdam conference, 152-4; confuses terms, 190; error of middle way, 193; misses real issue, 190; rejects capitalism and communism, 189
World on fire, 150
World War II, 200
Worship, moratorium, 150